C-2894　CAREER EXAMINATION SERIES

This is your
PASSBOOK for...

Media Specialist

Test Preparation Study Guide
Questions & Answers

COPYRIGHT NOTICE

This book is SOLELY intended for, is sold ONLY to, and its use is RESTRICTED to individual, bona fide applicants or candidates who qualify by virtue of having seriously filed applications for appropriate license, certificate, professional and/or promotional advancement, higher school matriculation, scholarship, or other legitimate requirements of education and/or governmental authorities.

This book is NOT intended for use, class instruction, tutoring, training, duplication, copying, reprinting, excerption, or adaptation, etc., by:

1) Other publishers
2) Proprietors and/or Instructors of "Coaching" and/or Preparatory Courses
3) Personnel and/or Training Divisions of commercial, industrial, and governmental organizations
4) Schools, colleges, or universities and/or their departments and staffs, including teachers and other personnel
5) Testing Agencies or Bureaus
6) Study groups which seek by the purchase of a single volume to copy and/or duplicate and/or adapt this material for use by the group as a whole without having purchased individual volumes for each of the members of the group
7) Et al.

Such persons would be in violation of appropriate Federal and State statutes.

PROVISION OF LICENSING AGREEMENTS – Recognized educational, commercial, industrial, and governmental institutions and organizations, and others legitimately engaged in educational pursuits, including training, testing, and measurement activities, may address request for a licensing agreement to the copyright owners, who will determine whether, and under what conditions, including fees and charges, the materials in this book may be used them. In other words, a licensing facility exists for the legitimate use of the material in this book on other than an individual basis. However, it is asseverated and affirmed here that the material in this book CANNOT be used without the receipt of the express permission of such a licensing agreement from the Publishers. Inquiries re licensing should be addressed to the company, attention rights and permissions department.

All rights reserved, including the right of reproduction in whole or in part, in any form or by any means, electronic or mechanical, including photocopying, recording, or by any information storage and retrieval system, without permission in writing from the Publisher.

Copyright © 2025 by
National Learning Corporation

212 Michael Drive, Syosset, NY 11791
(516) 921-8888 • www.passbooks.com
E-mail: info@passbooks.com

PASSBOOK® SERIES

THE *PASSBOOK® SERIES* has been created to prepare applicants and candidates for the ultimate academic battlefield – the examination room.

At some time in our lives, each and every one of us may be required to take an examination – for validation, matriculation, admission, qualification, registration, certification, or licensure.

Based on the assumption that every applicant or candidate has met the basic formal educational standards, has taken the required number of courses, and read the necessary texts, the *PASSBOOK® SERIES* furnishes the one special preparation which may assure passing with confidence, instead of failing with insecurity. Examination questions – together with answers – are furnished as the basic vehicle for study so that the mysteries of the examination and its compounding difficulties may be eliminated or diminished by a sure method.

This book is meant to help you pass your examination provided that you qualify and are serious in your objective.

The entire field is reviewed through the huge store of content information which is succinctly presented through a provocative and challenging approach – the question-and-answer method.

A climate of success is established by furnishing the correct answers at the end of each test.

You soon learn to recognize types of questions, forms of questions, and patterns of questioning. You may even begin to anticipate expected outcomes.

You perceive that many questions are repeated or adapted so that you can gain acute insights, which may enable you to score many sure points.

You learn how to confront new questions, or types of questions, and to attack them confidently and work out the correct answers.

You note objectives and emphases, and recognize pitfalls and dangers, so that you may make positive educational adjustments.

Moreover, you are kept fully informed in relation to new concepts, methods, practices, and directions in the field.

You discover that you are actually taking the examination all the time: you are preparing for the examination by "taking" an examination, not by reading extraneous and/or supererogatory textbooks.

In short, this PASSBOOK®, used directedly, should be an important factor in helping you to pass your test.

MEDIA SPECIALIST

DUTIES
Media Specialists, under direction, are responsible for writing promotional material and editing copy material prepared by subordinate staff. They assist in the design and production of material to convey information; provide technical and administrative supervision to subordinate staff; and maintain direct contact with a variety of media representatives to promote the use of materials. They advise program staff and local jurisdictions on production of materials.

SCOPE OF THE EXAMINATION
The written test will cover knowledge, skills and abilities in such areas as:

1. Preparing written material;
2. Principles of layout and design of printed publications; and
3. Proofreading.

HOW TO TAKE A TEST

I. YOU MUST PASS AN EXAMINATION

A. *WHAT EVERY CANDIDATE SHOULD KNOW*

Examination applicants often ask us for help in preparing for the written test. What can I study in advance? What kinds of questions will be asked? How will the test be given? How will the papers be graded?

As an applicant for a civil service examination, you may be wondering about some of these things. Our purpose here is to suggest effective methods of advance study and to describe civil service examinations.

Your chances for success on this examination can be increased if you know how to prepare. Those "pre-examination jitters" can be reduced if you know what to expect. You can even experience an adventure in good citizenship if you know why civil service exams are given.

B. *WHY ARE CIVIL SERVICE EXAMINATIONS GIVEN?*

Civil service examinations are important to you in two ways. As a citizen, you want public jobs filled by employees who know how to do their work. As a job seeker, you want a fair chance to compete for that job on an equal footing with other candidates. The best-known means of accomplishing this two-fold goal is the competitive examination.

Exams are widely publicized throughout the nation. They may be administered for jobs in federal, state, city, municipal, town or village governments or agencies.

Any citizen may apply, with some limitations, such as the age or residence of applicants. Your experience and education may be reviewed to see whether you meet the requirements for the particular examination. When these requirements exist, they are reasonable and applied consistently to all applicants. Thus, a competitive examination may cause you some uneasiness now, but it is your privilege and safeguard.

C. *HOW ARE CIVIL SERVICE EXAMS DEVELOPED?*

Examinations are carefully written by trained technicians who are specialists in the field known as "psychological measurement," in consultation with recognized authorities in the field of work that the test will cover. These experts recommend the subject matter areas or skills to be tested; only those knowledges or skills important to your success on the job are included. The most reliable books and source materials available are used as references. Together, the experts and technicians judge the difficulty level of the questions.

Test technicians know how to phrase questions so that the problem is clearly stated. Their ethics do not permit "trick" or "catch" questions. Questions may have been tried out on sample groups, or subjected to statistical analysis, to determine their usefulness.

Written tests are often used in combination with performance tests, ratings of training and experience, and oral interviews. All of these measures combine to form the best-known means of finding the right person for the right job.

II. HOW TO PASS THE WRITTEN TEST

A. NATURE OF THE EXAMINATION

To prepare intelligently for civil service examinations, you should know how they differ from school examinations you have taken. In school you were assigned certain definite pages to read or subjects to cover. The examination questions were quite detailed and usually emphasized memory. Civil service exams, on the other hand, try to discover your present ability to perform the duties of a position, plus your potentiality to learn these duties. In other words, a civil service exam attempts to predict how successful you will be. Questions cover such a broad area that they cannot be as minute and detailed as school exam questions.

In the public service similar kinds of work, or positions, are grouped together in one "class." This process is known as *position-classification*. All the positions in a class are paid according to the salary range for that class. One class title covers all of these positions, and they are all tested by the same examination.

B. FOUR BASIC STEPS

1) Study the announcement

How, then, can you know what subjects to study? Our best answer is: "Learn as much as possible about the class of positions for which you've applied." The exam will test the knowledge, skills and abilities needed to do the work.

Your most valuable source of information about the position you want is the official exam announcement. This announcement lists the training and experience qualifications. Check these standards and apply only if you come reasonably close to meeting them.

The brief description of the position in the examination announcement offers some clues to the subjects which will be tested. Think about the job itself. Review the duties in your mind. Can you perform them, or are there some in which you are rusty? Fill in the blank spots in your preparation.

Many jurisdictions preview the written test in the exam announcement by including a section called "Knowledge and Abilities Required," "Scope of the Examination," or some similar heading. Here you will find out specifically what fields will be tested.

2) Review your own background

Once you learn in general what the position is all about, and what you need to know to do the work, ask yourself which subjects you already know fairly well and which need improvement. You may wonder whether to concentrate on improving your strong areas or on building some background in your fields of weakness. When the announcement has specified "some knowledge" or "considerable knowledge," or has used adjectives like "beginning principles of..." or "advanced ... methods," you can get a clue as to the number and difficulty of questions to be asked in any given field. More questions, and hence broader coverage, would be included for those subjects which are more important in the work. Now weigh your strengths and weaknesses against the job requirements and prepare accordingly.

3) Determine the level of the position

Another way to tell how intensively you should prepare is to understand the level of the job for which you are applying. Is it the entering level? In other words, is this the position in which beginners in a field of work are hired? Or is it an intermediate or advanced level? Sometimes this is indicated by such words as "Junior" or "Senior" in the class title. Other jurisdictions use Roman numerals to designate the level – Clerk I, Clerk II, for example. The word "Supervisor" sometimes appears in the title. If the level is not indicated by the title, check the description of duties. Will you be working under very close supervision, or will you have responsibility for independent decisions in this work?

4) Choose appropriate study materials

Now that you know the subjects to be examined and the relative amount of each subject to be covered, you can choose suitable study materials. For beginning level jobs, or even advanced ones, if you have a pronounced weakness in some aspect of your training, read a modern, standard textbook in that field. Be sure it is up to date and has general coverage. Such books are normally available at your library, and the librarian will be glad to help you locate one. For entry-level positions, questions of appropriate difficulty are chosen – neither highly advanced questions, nor those too simple. Such questions require careful thought but not advanced training.

If the position for which you are applying is technical or advanced, you will read more advanced, specialized material. If you are already familiar with the basic principles of your field, elementary textbooks would waste your time. Concentrate on advanced textbooks and technical periodicals. Think through the concepts and review difficult problems in your field.

These are all general sources. You can get more ideas on your own initiative, following these leads. For example, training manuals and publications of the government agency which employs workers in your field can be useful, particularly for technical and professional positions. A letter or visit to the government department involved may result in more specific study suggestions, and certainly will provide you with a more definite idea of the exact nature of the position you are seeking.

III. KINDS OF TESTS

Tests are used for purposes other than measuring knowledge and ability to perform specified duties. For some positions, it is equally important to test ability to make adjustments to new situations or to profit from training. In others, basic mental abilities not dependent on information are essential. Questions which test these things may not appear as pertinent to the duties of the position as those which test for knowledge and information. Yet they are often highly important parts of a fair examination. For very general questions, it is almost impossible to help you direct your study efforts. What we can do is to point out some of the more common of these general abilities needed in public service positions and describe some typical questions.

1) General information

Broad, general information has been found useful for predicting job success in some kinds of work. This is tested in a variety of ways, from vocabulary lists to questions about current events. Basic background in some field of work, such as sociology or economics, may be sampled in a group of questions. Often these are principles which have become familiar to most persons through exposure rather than through formal training. It is difficult to advise you how to study for these questions; being alert to the world around you is our best suggestion.

2) Verbal ability

An example of an ability needed in many positions is verbal or language ability. Verbal ability is, in brief, the ability to use and understand words. Vocabulary and grammar tests are typical measures of this ability. Reading comprehension or paragraph interpretation questions are common in many kinds of civil service tests. You are given a paragraph of written material and asked to find its central meaning.

3) Numerical ability

Number skills can be tested by the familiar arithmetic problem, by checking paired lists of numbers to see which are alike and which are different, or by interpreting charts and graphs. In the latter test, a graph may be printed in the test booklet which you are asked to use as the basis for answering questions.

4) Observation

A popular test for law-enforcement positions is the observation test. A picture is shown to you for several minutes, then taken away. Questions about the picture test your ability to observe both details and larger elements.

5) Following directions

In many positions in the public service, the employee must be able to carry out written instructions dependably and accurately. You may be given a chart with several columns, each column listing a variety of information. The questions require you to carry out directions involving the information given in the chart.

6) Skills and aptitudes

Performance tests effectively measure some manual skills and aptitudes. When the skill is one in which you are trained, such as typing or shorthand, you can practice. These tests are often very much like those given in business school or high school courses. For many of the other skills and aptitudes, however, no short-time preparation can be made. Skills and abilities natural to you or that you have developed throughout your lifetime are being tested.

Many of the general questions just described provide all the data needed to answer the questions and ask you to use your reasoning ability to find the answers. Your best preparation for these tests, as well as for tests of facts and ideas, is to be at your physical and mental best. You, no doubt, have your own methods of getting into an exam-taking mood and keeping "in shape." The next section lists some ideas on this subject.

IV. KINDS OF QUESTIONS

Only rarely is the "essay" question, which you answer in narrative form, used in civil service tests. Civil service tests are usually of the short-answer type. Full instructions for answering these questions will be given to you at the examination. But in case this is your first experience with short-answer questions and separate answer sheets, here is what you need to know:

1) Multiple-choice Questions

Most popular of the short-answer questions is the "multiple choice" or "best answer" question. It can be used, for example, to test for factual knowledge, ability to solve problems or judgment in meeting situations found at work.

A multiple-choice question is normally one of three types—
- It can begin with an incomplete statement followed by several possible endings. You are to find the one ending which *best* completes the statement, although some of the others may not be entirely wrong.
- It can also be a complete statement in the form of a question which is answered by choosing one of the statements listed.

- It can be in the form of a problem – again you select the best answer.

Here is an example of a multiple-choice question with a discussion which should give you some clues as to the method for choosing the right answer:

When an employee has a complaint about his assignment, the action which will *best* help him overcome his difficulty is to
   A. discuss his difficulty with his coworkers
   B. take the problem to the head of the organization
   C. take the problem to the person who gave him the assignment
   D. say nothing to anyone about his complaint

In answering this question, you should study each of the choices to find which is best. Consider choice "A" – Certainly an employee may discuss his complaint with fellow employees, but no change or improvement can result, and the complaint remains unresolved. Choice "B" is a poor choice since the head of the organization probably does not know what assignment you have been given, and taking your problem to him is known as "going over the head" of the supervisor. The supervisor, or person who made the assignment, is the person who can clarify it or correct any injustice. Choice "C" is, therefore, correct. To say nothing, as in choice "D," is unwise. Supervisors have and interest in knowing the problems employees are facing, and the employee is seeking a solution to his problem.

2) True/False Questions

The "true/false" or "right/wrong" form of question is sometimes used. Here a complete statement is given. Your job is to decide whether the statement is right or wrong.

SAMPLE: A roaming cell-phone call to a nearby city costs less than a non-roaming call to a distant city.

This statement is wrong, or false, since roaming calls are more expensive.

This is not a complete list of all possible question forms, although most of the others are variations of these common types. You will always get complete directions for answering questions. Be sure you understand *how* to mark your answers – ask questions until you do.

V. RECORDING YOUR ANSWERS

Computer terminals are used more and more today for many different kinds of exams.

For an examination with very few applicants, you may be told to record your answers in the test booklet itself. Separate answer sheets are much more common. If this separate answer sheet is to be scored by machine – and this is often the case – it is highly important that you mark your answers correctly in order to get credit.

An electronic scoring machine is often used in civil service offices because of the speed with which papers can be scored. Machine-scored answer sheets must be marked with a pencil, which will be given to you. This pencil has a high graphite content which responds to the electronic scoring machine. As a matter of fact, stray dots may register as answers, so do not let your pencil rest on the answer sheet while you are pondering the correct answer. Also, if your pencil lead breaks or is otherwise defective, ask for another.

Since the answer sheet will be dropped in a slot in the scoring machine, be careful not to bend the corners or get the paper crumpled.

The answer sheet normally has five vertical columns of numbers, with 30 numbers to a column. These numbers correspond to the question numbers in your test booklet. After each number, going across the page are four or five pairs of dotted lines. These short dotted lines have small letters or numbers above them. The first two pairs may also have a "T" or "F" above the letters. This indicates that the first two pairs only are to be used if the questions are of the true-false type. If the questions are multiple choice, disregard the "T" and "F" and pay attention only to the small letters or numbers.

Answer your questions in the manner of the sample that follows:

32. The largest city in the United States is
    A. Washington, D.C.
    B. New York City
    C. Chicago
    D. Detroit
    E. San Francisco

1) Choose the answer you think is best. (New York City is the largest, so "B" is correct.)
2) Find the row of dotted lines numbered the same as the question you are answering. (Find row number 32)
3) Find the pair of dotted lines corresponding to the answer. (Find the pair of lines under the mark "B.")
4) Make a solid black mark between the dotted lines.

VI. BEFORE THE TEST

Common sense will help you find procedures to follow to get ready for an examination. Too many of us, however, overlook these sensible measures. Indeed, nervousness and fatigue have been found to be the most serious reasons why applicants fail to do their best on civil service tests. Here is a list of reminders:

- Begin your preparation early – Don't wait until the last minute to go scurrying around for books and materials or to find out what the position is all about.
- Prepare continuously – An hour a night for a week is better than an all-night cram session. This has been definitely established. What is more, a night a week for a month will return better dividends than crowding your study into a shorter period of time.
- Locate the place of the exam – You have been sent a notice telling you when and where to report for the examination. If the location is in a different town or otherwise unfamiliar to you, it would be well to inquire the best route and learn something about the building.
- Relax the night before the test – Allow your mind to rest. Do not study at all that night. Plan some mild recreation or diversion; then go to bed early and get a good night's sleep.
- Get up early enough to make a leisurely trip to the place for the test – This way unforeseen events, traffic snarls, unfamiliar buildings, etc. will not upset you.
- Dress comfortably – A written test is not a fashion show. You will be known by number and not by name, so wear something comfortable.

- Leave excess paraphernalia at home – Shopping bags and odd bundles will get in your way. You need bring only the items mentioned in the official notice you received; usually everything you need is provided. Do not bring reference books to the exam. They will only confuse those last minutes and be taken away from you when in the test room.
- Arrive somewhat ahead of time – If because of transportation schedules you must get there very early, bring a newspaper or magazine to take your mind off yourself while waiting.
- Locate the examination room – When you have found the proper room, you will be directed to the seat or part of the room where you will sit. Sometimes you are given a sheet of instructions to read while you are waiting. Do not fill out any forms until you are told to do so; just read them and be prepared.
- Relax and prepare to listen to the instructions
- If you have any physical problem that may keep you from doing your best, be sure to tell the test administrator. If you are sick or in poor health, you really cannot do your best on the exam. You can come back and take the test some other time.

VII. AT THE TEST

The day of the test is here and you have the test booklet in your hand. The temptation to get going is very strong. Caution! There is more to success than knowing the right answers. You must know how to identify your papers and understand variations in the type of short-answer question used in this particular examination. Follow these suggestions for maximum results from your efforts:

1) Cooperate with the monitor
The test administrator has a duty to create a situation in which you can be as much at ease as possible. He will give instructions, tell you when to begin, check to see that you are marking your answer sheet correctly, and so on. He is not there to guard you, although he will see that your competitors do not take unfair advantage. He wants to help you do your best.

2) Listen to all instructions
Don't jump the gun! Wait until you understand all directions. In most civil service tests you get more time than you need to answer the questions. So don't be in a hurry. Read each word of instructions until you clearly understand the meaning. Study the examples, listen to all announcements and follow directions. Ask questions if you do not understand what to do.

3) Identify your papers
Civil service exams are usually identified by number only. You will be assigned a number; you must not put your name on your test papers. Be sure to copy your number correctly. Since more than one exam may be given, copy your exact examination title.

4) Plan your time
Unless you are told that a test is a "speed" or "rate of work" test, speed itself is usually not important. Time enough to answer all the questions will be provided, but this does not mean that you have all day. An overall time limit has been set. Divide the total time (in minutes) by the number of questions to determine the approximate time you have for each question.

5) Do not linger over difficult questions

If you come across a difficult question, mark it with a paper clip (useful to have along) and come back to it when you have been through the booklet. One caution if you do this – be sure to skip a number on your answer sheet as well. Check often to be sure that you have not lost your place and that you are marking in the row numbered the same as the question you are answering.

6) Read the questions

Be sure you know what the question asks! Many capable people are unsuccessful because they failed to *read* the questions correctly.

7) Answer all questions

Unless you have been instructed that a penalty will be deducted for incorrect answers, it is better to guess than to omit a question.

8) Speed tests

It is often better NOT to guess on speed tests. It has been found that on timed tests people are tempted to spend the last few seconds before time is called in marking answers at random – without even reading them – in the hope of picking up a few extra points. To discourage this practice, the instructions may warn you that your score will be "corrected" for guessing. That is, a penalty will be applied. The incorrect answers will be deducted from the correct ones, or some other penalty formula will be used.

9) Review your answers

If you finish before time is called, go back to the questions you guessed or omitted to give them further thought. Review other answers if you have time.

10) Return your test materials

If you are ready to leave before others have finished or time is called, take ALL your materials to the monitor and leave quietly. Never take any test material with you. The monitor can discover whose papers are not complete, and taking a test booklet may be grounds for disqualification.

VIII. EXAMINATION TECHNIQUES

1) Read the general instructions carefully. These are usually printed on the first page of the exam booklet. As a rule, these instructions refer to the timing of the examination; the fact that you should not start work until the signal and must stop work at a signal, etc. If there are any *special* instructions, such as a choice of questions to be answered, make sure that you note this instruction carefully.

2) When you are ready to start work on the examination, that is as soon as the signal has been given, read the instructions to each question booklet, underline any key words or phrases, such as *least, best, outline, describe* and the like. In this way you will tend to answer as requested rather than discover on reviewing your paper that you *listed without describing*, that you selected the *worst* choice rather than the *best* choice, etc.

3) If the examination is of the objective or multiple-choice type – that is, each question will also give a series of possible answers: A, B, C or D, and you are called upon to select the best answer and write the letter next to that answer on your answer paper – it is advisable to start answering each question in turn. There may be anywhere from 50 to 100 such questions in the three or four hours allotted and you can see how much time would be taken if you read through all the questions before beginning to answer any. Furthermore, if you come across a question or group of questions which you know would be difficult to answer, it would undoubtedly affect your handling of all the other questions.

4) If the examination is of the essay type and contains but a few questions, it is a moot point as to whether you should read all the questions before starting to answer any one. Of course, if you are given a choice – say five out of seven and the like – then it is essential to read all the questions so you can eliminate the two that are most difficult. If, however, you are asked to answer all the questions, there may be danger in trying to answer the easiest one first because you may find that you will spend too much time on it. The best technique is to answer the first question, then proceed to the second, etc.

5) Time your answers. Before the exam begins, write down the time it started, then add the time allowed for the examination and write down the time it must be completed, then divide the time available somewhat as follows:
    - If 3-1/2 hours are allowed, that would be 210 minutes. If you have 80 objective-type questions, that would be an average of 2-1/2 minutes per question. Allow yourself no more than 2 minutes per question, or a total of 160 minutes, which will permit about 50 minutes to review.
    - If for the time allotment of 210 minutes there are 7 essay questions to answer, that would average about 30 minutes a question. Give yourself only 25 minutes per question so that you have about 35 minutes to review.

6) The most important instruction is to *read each question* and make sure you know what is wanted. The second most important instruction is to *time yourself properly* so that you answer every question. The third most important instruction is to *answer every question*. Guess if you have to but include something for each question. Remember that you will receive no credit for a blank and will probably receive some credit if you write something in answer to an essay question. If you guess a letter – say "B" for a multiple-choice question – you may have guessed right. If you leave a blank as an answer to a multiple-choice question, the examiners may respect your feelings but it will not add a point to your score. Some exams may penalize you for wrong answers, so in such cases *only*, you may not want to guess unless you have some basis for your answer.

7) Suggestions
    a. Objective-type questions
        1. Examine the question booklet for proper sequence of pages and questions
        2. Read all instructions carefully
        3. Skip any question which seems too difficult; return to it after all other questions have been answered
        4. Apportion your time properly; do not spend too much time on any single question or group of questions

5. Note and underline key words – *all, most, fewest, least, best, worst, same, opposite,* etc.
6. Pay particular attention to negatives
7. Note unusual option, e.g., unduly long, short, complex, different or similar in content to the body of the question
8. Observe the use of "hedging" words – *probably, may, most likely,* etc.
9. Make sure that your answer is put next to the same number as the question
10. Do not second-guess unless you have good reason to believe the second answer is definitely more correct
11. Cross out original answer if you decide another answer is more accurate; do not erase until you are ready to hand your paper in
12. Answer all questions; guess unless instructed otherwise
13. Leave time for review

b. Essay questions
1. Read each question carefully
2. Determine exactly what is wanted. Underline key words or phrases.
3. Decide on outline or paragraph answer
4. Include many different points and elements unless asked to develop any one or two points or elements
5. Show impartiality by giving pros and cons unless directed to select one side only
6. Make and write down any assumptions you find necessary to answer the questions
7. Watch your English, grammar, punctuation and choice of words
8. Time your answers; don't crowd material

8) Answering the essay question

Most essay questions can be answered by framing the specific response around several key words or ideas. Here are a few such key words or ideas:

M's: manpower, materials, methods, money, management
P's: purpose, program, policy, plan, procedure, practice, problems, pitfalls, personnel, public relations

a. Six basic steps in handling problems:
1. Preliminary plan and background development
2. Collect information, data and facts
3. Analyze and interpret information, data and facts
4. Analyze and develop solutions as well as make recommendations
5. Prepare report and sell recommendations
6. Install recommendations and follow up effectiveness

b. Pitfalls to avoid
1. *Taking things for granted* – A statement of the situation does not necessarily imply that each of the elements is necessarily true; for example, a complaint may be invalid and biased so that all that can be taken for granted is that a complaint has been registered

2. *Considering only one side of a situation* – Wherever possible, indicate several alternatives and then point out the reasons you selected the best one
3. *Failing to indicate follow up* – Whenever your answer indicates action on your part, make certain that you will take proper follow-up action to see how successful your recommendations, procedures or actions turn out to be
4. *Taking too long in answering any single question* – Remember to time your answers properly

IX. AFTER THE TEST

Scoring procedures differ in detail among civil service jurisdictions although the general principles are the same. Whether the papers are hand-scored or graded by machine we have described, they are nearly always graded by number. That is, the person who marks the paper knows only the number – never the name – of the applicant. Not until all the papers have been graded will they be matched with names. If other tests, such as training and experience or oral interview ratings have been given, scores will be combined. Different parts of the examination usually have different weights. For example, the written test might count 60 percent of the final grade, and a rating of training and experience 40 percent. In many jurisdictions, veterans will have a certain number of points added to their grades.

After the final grade has been determined, the names are placed in grade order and an eligible list is established. There are various methods for resolving ties between those who get the same final grade – probably the most common is to place first the name of the person whose application was received first. Job offers are made from the eligible list in the order the names appear on it. You will be notified of your grade and your rank as soon as all these computations have been made. This will be done as rapidly as possible.

People who are found to meet the requirements in the announcement are called "eligibles." Their names are put on a list of eligible candidates. An eligible's chances of getting a job depend on how high he stands on this list and how fast agencies are filling jobs from the list.

When a job is to be filled from a list of eligibles, the agency asks for the names of people on the list of eligibles for that job. When the civil service commission receives this request, it sends to the agency the names of the three people highest on this list. Or, if the job to be filled has specialized requirements, the office sends the agency the names of the top three persons who meet these requirements from the general list.

The appointing officer makes a choice from among the three people whose names were sent to him. If the selected person accepts the appointment, the names of the others are put back on the list to be considered for future openings.

That is the rule in hiring from all kinds of eligible lists, whether they are for typist, carpenter, chemist, or something else. For every vacancy, the appointing officer has his choice of any one of the top three eligibles on the list. This explains why the person whose name is on top of the list sometimes does not get an appointment when some of the persons lower on the list do. If the appointing officer chooses the second or third eligible, the No. 1 eligible does not get a job at once, but stays on the list until he is appointed or the list is terminated.

X. HOW TO PASS THE INTERVIEW TEST

The examination for which you applied requires an oral interview test. You have already taken the written test and you are now being called for the interview test – the final part of the formal examination.

You may think that it is not possible to prepare for an interview test and that there are no procedures to follow during an interview. Our purpose is to point out some things you can do in advance that will help you and some good rules to follow and pitfalls to avoid while you are being interviewed.

What is an interview supposed to test?

The written examination is designed to test the technical knowledge and competence of the candidate; the oral is designed to evaluate intangible qualities, not readily measured otherwise, and to establish a list showing the relative fitness of each candidate – as measured against his competitors – for the position sought. Scoring is not on the basis of "right" and "wrong," but on a sliding scale of values ranging from "not passable" to "outstanding." As a matter of fact, it is possible to achieve a relatively low score without a single "incorrect" answer because of evident weakness in the qualities being measured.

Occasionally, an examination may consist entirely of an oral test – either an individual or a group oral. In such cases, information is sought concerning the technical knowledges and abilities of the candidate, since there has been no written examination for this purpose. More commonly, however, an oral test is used to supplement a written examination.

Who conducts interviews?

The composition of oral boards varies among different jurisdictions. In nearly all, a representative of the personnel department serves as chairman. One of the members of the board may be a representative of the department in which the candidate would work. In some cases, "outside experts" are used, and, frequently, a businessman or some other representative of the general public is asked to serve. Labor and management or other special groups may be represented. The aim is to secure the services of experts in the appropriate field.

However the board is composed, it is a good idea (and not at all improper or unethical) to ascertain in advance of the interview who the members are and what groups they represent. When you are introduced to them, you will have some idea of their backgrounds and interests, and at least you will not stutter and stammer over their names.

What should be done before the interview?

While knowledge about the board members is useful and takes some of the surprise element out of the interview, there is other preparation which is more substantive. It *is* possible to prepare for an oral interview – in several ways:

1) Keep a copy of your application and review it carefully before the interview

This may be the only document before the oral board, and the starting point of the interview. Know what education and experience you have listed there, and the sequence and dates of all of it. Sometimes the board will ask you to review the highlights of your experience for them; you should not have to hem and haw doing it.

2) Study the class specification and the examination announcement

Usually, the oral board has one or both of these to guide them. The qualities, characteristics or knowledges required by the position sought are stated in these documents. They offer valuable clues as to the nature of the oral interview. For example, if the job involves supervisory responsibilities, the announcement will usually indicate that knowledge of modern supervisory methods and the qualifications of the candidate as a supervisor will be tested. If so, you can expect such questions, frequently in the form of a hypothetical situation which you are expected to solve. NEVER go into an oral without knowledge of the duties and responsibilities of the job you seek.

3) Think through each qualification required

Try to visualize the kind of questions you would ask if you were a board member. How well could you answer them? Try especially to appraise your own knowledge and background in each area, *measured against the job sought*, and identify any areas in which you are weak. Be critical and realistic – do not flatter yourself.

4) Do some general reading in areas in which you feel you may be weak

For example, if the job involves supervision and your past experience has NOT, some general reading in supervisory methods and practices, particularly in the field of human relations, might be useful. Do NOT study agency procedures or detailed manuals. The oral board will be testing your understanding and capacity, not your memory.

5) Get a good night's sleep and watch your general health and mental attitude

You will want a clear head at the interview. Take care of a cold or any other minor ailment, and of course, no hangovers.

What should be done on the day of the interview?

Now comes the day of the interview itself. Give yourself plenty of time to get there. Plan to arrive somewhat ahead of the scheduled time, particularly if your appointment is in the fore part of the day. If a previous candidate fails to appear, the board might be ready for you a bit early. By early afternoon an oral board is almost invariably behind schedule if there are many candidates, and you may have to wait. Take along a book or magazine to read, or your application to review, but leave any extraneous material in the waiting room when you go in for your interview. In any event, relax and compose yourself.

The matter of dress is important. The board is forming impressions about you – from your experience, your manners, your attitude, and your appearance. Give your personal appearance careful attention. Dress your best, but not your flashiest. Choose conservative, appropriate clothing, and be sure it is immaculate. This is a business interview, and your appearance should indicate that you regard it as such. Besides, being well groomed and properly dressed will help boost your confidence.

Sooner or later, someone will call your name and escort you into the interview room. *This is it.* From here on you are on your own. It is too late for any more preparation. But remember, you asked for this opportunity to prove your fitness, and you are here because your request was granted.

What happens when you go in?

The usual sequence of events will be as follows: The clerk (who is often the board stenographer) will introduce you to the chairman of the oral board, who will introduce you to the other members of the board. Acknowledge the introductions before you sit down. Do not be surprised if you find a microphone facing you or a stenotypist sitting by. Oral interviews are usually recorded in the event of an appeal or other review.

Usually the chairman of the board will open the interview by reviewing the highlights of your education and work experience from your application – primarily for the benefit of the other members of the board, as well as to get the material into the record. Do not interrupt or comment unless there is an error or significant misinterpretation; if that is the case, do not hesitate. But do not quibble about insignificant matters. Also, he will usually ask you some question about your education, experience or your present job – partly to get you to start talking and to establish the interviewing "rapport." He may start the actual questioning, or turn it over to one of the other members. Frequently, each member undertakes the questioning on a particular area, one in which he is perhaps most competent, so you can expect each member to participate in the examination. Because time is limited, you may also expect some rather abrupt switches in the direction the questioning takes, so do not be upset by it. Normally, a board member will not pursue a single line of questioning unless he discovers a particular strength or weakness.

After each member has participated, the chairman will usually ask whether any member has any further questions, then will ask you if you have anything you wish to add. Unless you are expecting this question, it may floor you. Worse, it may start you off on an extended, extemporaneous speech. The board is not usually seeking more information. The question is principally to offer you a last opportunity to present further qualifications or to indicate that you have nothing to add. So, if you feel that a significant qualification or characteristic has been overlooked, it is proper to point it out in a sentence or so. Do not compliment the board on the thoroughness of their examination – they have been sketchy, and you know it. If you wish, merely say, "No thank you, I have nothing further to add." This is a point where you can "talk yourself out" of a good impression or fail to present an important bit of information. Remember, *you close the interview yourself.*

The chairman will then say, "That is all, Mr. _____, thank you." Do not be startled; the interview is over, and quicker than you think. Thank him, gather your belongings and take your leave. Save your sigh of relief for the other side of the door.

How to put your best foot forward

Throughout this entire process, you may feel that the board individually and collectively is trying to pierce your defenses, seek out your hidden weaknesses and embarrass and confuse you. Actually, this is not true. They are obliged to make an appraisal of your qualifications for the job you are seeking, and they want to see you in your best light. Remember, they must interview all candidates and a non-cooperative candidate may become a failure in spite of their best efforts to bring out his qualifications. Here are 15 suggestions that will help you:

1) **Be natural – Keep your attitude confident, not cocky**

If you are not confident that you can do the job, do not expect the board to be. Do not apologize for your weaknesses, try to bring out your strong points. The board is interested in a positive, not negative, presentation. Cockiness will antagonize any board member and make him wonder if you are covering up a weakness by a false show of strength.

2) **Get comfortable, but don't lounge or sprawl**

Sit erectly but not stiffly. A careless posture may lead the board to conclude that you are careless in other things, or at least that you are not impressed by the importance of the occasion. Either conclusion is natural, even if incorrect. Do not fuss with your clothing, a pencil or an ashtray. Your hands may occasionally be useful to emphasize a point; do not let them become a point of distraction.

3) **Do not wisecrack or make small talk**

This is a serious situation, and your attitude should show that you consider it as such. Further, the time of the board is limited – they do not want to waste it, and neither should you.

4) Do not exaggerate your experience or abilities

In the first place, from information in the application or other interviews and sources, the board may know more about you than you think. Secondly, you probably will not get away with it. An experienced board is rather adept at spotting such a situation, so do not take the chance.

5) If you know a board member, do not make a point of it, yet do not hide it

Certainly you are not fooling him, and probably not the other members of the board. Do not try to take advantage of your acquaintanceship – it will probably do you little good.

6) Do not dominate the interview

Let the board do that. They will give you the clues – do not assume that you have to do all the talking. Realize that the board has a number of questions to ask you, and do not try to take up all the interview time by showing off your extensive knowledge of the answer to the first one.

7) Be attentive

You only have 20 minutes or so, and you should keep your attention at its sharpest throughout. When a member is addressing a problem or question to you, give him your undivided attention. Address your reply principally to him, but do not exclude the other board members.

8) Do not interrupt

A board member may be stating a problem for you to analyze. He will ask you a question when the time comes. Let him state the problem, and wait for the question.

9) Make sure you understand the question

Do not try to answer until you are sure what the question is. If it is not clear, restate it in your own words or ask the board member to clarify it for you. However, do not haggle about minor elements.

10) Reply promptly but not hastily

A common entry on oral board rating sheets is "candidate responded readily," or "candidate hesitated in replies." Respond as promptly and quickly as you can, but do not jump to a hasty, ill-considered answer.

11) Do not be peremptory in your answers

A brief answer is proper – but do not fire your answer back. That is a losing game from your point of view. The board member can probably ask questions much faster than you can answer them.

12) Do not try to create the answer you think the board member wants

He is interested in what kind of mind you have and how it works – not in playing games. Furthermore, he can usually spot this practice and will actually grade you down on it.

13) Do not switch sides in your reply merely to agree with a board member

Frequently, a member will take a contrary position merely to draw you out and to see if you are willing and able to defend your point of view. Do not start a debate, yet do not surrender a good position. If a position is worth taking, it is worth defending.

14) Do not be afraid to admit an error in judgment if you are shown to be wrong

The board knows that you are forced to reply without any opportunity for careful consideration. Your answer may be demonstrably wrong. If so, admit it and get on with the interview.

15) Do not dwell at length on your present job

The opening question may relate to your present assignment. Answer the question but do not go into an extended discussion. You are being examined for a *new* job, not your present one. As a matter of fact, try to phrase ALL your answers in terms of the job for which you are being examined.

Basis of Rating

Probably you will forget most of these "do's" and "don'ts" when you walk into the oral interview room. Even remembering them all will not ensure you a passing grade. Perhaps you did not have the qualifications in the first place. But remembering them will help you to put your best foot forward, without treading on the toes of the board members.

Rumor and popular opinion to the contrary notwithstanding, an oral board wants you to make the best appearance possible. They know you are under pressure – but they also want to see how you respond to it as a guide to what your reaction would be under the pressures of the job you seek. They will be influenced by the degree of poise you display, the personal traits you show and the manner in which you respond.

ABOUT THIS BOOK

This book contains tests divided into Examination Sections. Go through each test, answering every question in the margin. We have also attached a sample answer sheet at the back of the book that can be removed and used. At the end of each test look at the answer key and check your answers. On the ones you got wrong, look at the right answer choice and learn. Do not fill in the answers first. Do not memorize the questions and answers, but understand the answer and principles involved. On your test, the questions will likely be different from the samples. Questions are changed and new ones added. If you understand these past questions you should have success with any changes that arise. Tests may consist of several types of questions. We have additional books on each subject should more study be advisable or necessary for you. Finally, the more you study, the better prepared you will be. This book is intended to be the last thing you study before you walk into the examination room. Prior study of relevant texts is also recommended. NLC publishes some of these in our Fundamental Series. Knowledge and good sense are important factors in passing your exam. Good luck also helps. So now study this Passbook, absorb the material contained within and take that knowledge into the examination. Then do your best to pass that exam.

EXAMINATION SECTION

EXAMINATION SECTION
TEST 1

DIRECTIONS: Each question or incomplete statement is followed by several suggested answers or completions. Select the one that BEST answers the question or completes the statement. *PRINT THE LETTER OF THE CORRECT ANSWER IN THE SPACE AT THE RIGHT.*

1. Of the following, the order in which a piece of local copy is MOST likely to flow is
    A. city editor, copy reader, compositor
    B. compositor, city editor, copy reader
    C. compositor, copy reader, city editor
    D. copy reader, compositor, city editor

    1.____

2. The one who edits copy and writes headlines at a newspaper copy desk is USUALLY called a
    A. copy cutter   B. copy holder   C. copy editor   D. layout tech

    2.____

3. An editorial assistant is asked to contact a representative of a cosmetics company for general information about a product that will be featured in an upcoming lifestyle feature. The assistant arranges a video call with an influencer who has promoted the product on Instagram. This is _____ because _____.
    A. *appropriate*; the influencer needs to know the product in depth in order to heavily promote it
    B. *appropriate*; influencers are typically employed by the businesses they promote and are representatives of the company
    C. *inappropriate*; influencers as a whole cannot be trusted
    D. *inappropriate*; influencers are typically not affiliated with the businesses they promote and are not representatives of the company

    3.____

4. As a defense against libel, one could claim that a statement was quoted from the CONGRESSIONAL RECORD and, therefore, was a(n)
    A. indirect quotation   B. personal comment
    C. privileged statement   D. reporter's prerogative

    4.____

5. In order to have an illustration continue off the edge of a page, you would instruct the printer to
    A. bleed   B. cutoff   C. justify   D. mortise

    5.____

6. The description that accompanies a photograph or diagram is called a(n)
    A. cutline   B. flag   C. overhead   D. underhead

    6.____

7. A headline stretching across all columns of a page is called a
    A. bank   B. banner   C. cross line   D. drop line

    7.____

8. You would expect a headline that is flush right and left to
   A. comprise two or more decks
   B. fill the entire line
   C. have black em borders at both ends
   D. have two ems of white space on both left and right hand sides

9. A headline that carries a story continued from another page is known as a
   A. break   B. filler   C. jump   D. read-in

10. The secondary part of a headline is a
    A. byline   B. deck   C. slug   D. subhead

11. A single piece of type that includes two or more letters is called
    A. dingbat   B. linotype   C. logotype   D. nonpareil

12. The one of the following terms that refers to the stylized name of a newspaper or magazine on the publication's first page is
    A. block   B. mast   C. title   D. flag

13. Type left over and unused after a magazine has been sent to press is called
    A. folo copy   B. make-ready   C. overset   D. quoin

14. An upper and lower case crossline reads as follows: Dr. Doe Appointed.
    The unit count of this crossline is
    A. 14½   B. 16   C. 18   D. 19

15. An editor reads the following sentence: "Dr. Perry's wife Margie said the longtime pediatrician was proud to be apart of the West Lake community."
    The editor should revise this sentence because
    A. family members should not be quoted unless absolutely necessary
    B. the sentence should be in the present tense
    C. using "Dr. Perry" and "pediatrician" is redundant
    D. there is a misspelling

16. When copy for a standard-size newspaper is returned with instructions to *cut to 1 col.*, the number of words should be reduced to APPROXIMATELY
    A. 500   B. 1000   C. 1500   D. 2000

17. A proofreader writes and circles the abbreviation *sc* in the margin, meaning that the text should be
    A. bold   B. resized   C. stricken   D. set in small caps

18. When a story is continued on a second page, the copyreader marks the bottom of the first page with
    A. ##   B. -30-   C. insuff.   D. more

19. The copyreader's symbol which is used to indicate that a subhead should be centered is
    A. ⌐   B. ⌙   C. ⌙⌐   D. ⌐⌙

20. The copyreader's symbol which is used to indicate the start of a paragraph is 20.____

A. ⌐ B. # C. ◯ D. ∼

Questions 21-25.

DIRECTIONS: Questions 21 through 25 consist of four pairs of words each. Some of the words are spelled correctly; others are spelled incorrectly. For each question, indicate in the space at the right the letter preceding that pair of words in which BOTH words are spelled CORRECTLY.

21. A. hygienic, inviegle B. omniscience, pittance 21.____
    C. plagarize, nullify D. seargent, perilous

22. A. auxilary, existence B. pronounciation, baccalaureate 22.____
    C. ignominy, indegence D. suable, baccalaureate

23. A. discreet, inaudible B. hypocricy, onerous 23.____
    C. liquidate, maintainance D. transparancy, onerous

24. A. facility, stimulent B. frugel, sanitary 24.____
    C. monetary, prefatory D. punctileous, credentials

25. A. bankruptsy, perceptible B. disuade, resilient 25.____
    C. exhilerate, expectancy D. panegyric, disparate

KEY (CORRECT ANSWERS)

1.	A	11.	C
2.	C	12.	D
3.	D	13.	C
4.	C	14.	B
5.	A	15.	D
6.	A	16.	B
7.	B	17.	D
8.	B	18.	D
9.	C	19.	C
10.	B	20.	A

21.	B
22.	D
23.	A
24.	C
25.	D

TEST 2

DIRECTIONS: Each question or incomplete statement is followed by several suggested answers or completions. Select the one that BEST answers the question or completes the statement. *PRINT THE LETTER OF THE CORRECT ANSWER IN THE SPACE AT THE RIGHT.*

1. Spot news stories are USUALLY written 1.____
   A. as feature articles
   B. in inverted pyramid style
   C. to fill inside pages
   D. with chronological organization

2. Which of the following contains no punctuation or grammar error?
   A. Adams the second American president, hailed from Massachusetts.
   B. Grant's-Tomb can be found in Manhattan near the Hudson River.
   C. Washington's Mount Vernon, is set on a hill near the Potomac.
   D. Jefferson's estate, Monticello, is located in Virginia.

3. A good reporter avoids taking extensive notes during an interview because 3.____
   A. accuracy is of secondary importance in reporting an interview
   B. a rewrite editor may actually write the story
   C. this may mark the reporter as an amateur
   D. this may distract the person being interviewed

4. A reporter is present at a function where a distinguished person is scheduled to speak. He has a complete advance copy of the text. 4.____
   During the speech, the reporter could BEST use his time to
   A. follow the text to see if the speaker deviates from it
   B. organize the material of the text for later writing
   C. take direct quotations from the text
   D. write headlines for the story

5. A news story written in an inverted pyramid form is one in which the 5.____
   A. climax is reached at the end of the story
   B. climax is reached near the middle of the story
   C. facts are arranged in chronological order of occurrence
   D. facts are arranged in descending order of reader interest

6. According to the AP Stylebook, in a news story, the first mention of the former Catholic Cardinal of New York should be written as 6.____
   A. Cardinal Terence Cook
   B. Terence Cardinal Cook
   C. The Rt. Rev. Terence Cook
   D. The Very Rev. Terence Cook

7. Of the following pairs, the one that is an example of a homophone is 7.____
   A. sing; sang
   B. ring (verb); ring (noun)
   C. inside; outside
   D. baring; bearing

4

8. The MOST common type of lede on newspaper stories is the _____ lede.
   A. astonisher B. quotation
   C. summary   D. suspended-interest

9. The one of the following terms which does NOT designate a story accompanying a report of a major news event is
   A. precede   B. shirt tail   C. sidebar   D. subhead

10. A second-day story is also known as a
    A. filler   B. flimsy
    C. follow copy D. follow story

11. A phrase or word used on copy to identify additional pages of a news story is called a
    A. headline   B. slot   C. slug   D. stamp

12. A *tear sheet* is a
    A. carbon copy of a story   B. galley proof of a story
    C. page proof of a publication D. printed page from a publication

13. If you were told to *boil* a story, you would
    A. expand with editorial comment   B. present only essential facts
    C. try to keep it a *scoop*   D. write a large headline spread

14. If a reporter went to the *morgue*, he would be seeing
    A. carbon copies of an article he had just written
    B. clippings on the subject he was writing about
    C. galley proofs of a recently completed article
    D. incoming press association teletype copy

15. A beat reporter's *future book* is a
    A. chronological listing on expected events on his beat
    B. list of news sources on his beat
    C. novel he eventually hopes to write
    D. schedule of assignments kept for editor of editorial page

16. To a magazine editor, the term *query* means a
    A. letter outlining an article idea
    B. personal request for conference with the editor
    C. request for an advance
    D. rough draft of an article

17. The one of the following that is NOT on the editorial staff of a large metropolitan newspaper is the
    A. copyreader   B. photographer
    C. proofreader D. rewrite man

18. The name given to a newspaper contributor who writes, edits or provides photography on a freelance basis is
    A. bulldog   B. beat   C. stringer   D. pooler

19. A writer is assigned to cover the local school district. In this case, the school district is known as the writer's
    A. territory   B. beat   C. press pool   D. lead

20. Information that is no longer under copyright protection is considered part of the
    A. free press
    B. free speech entitlement
    C. public record
    D. public domain

KEY (CORRECT ANSWERS)

1.	B	11.	C
2.	D	12.	D
3.	D	13.	B
4.	A	14.	B
5.	D	15.	A
6.	A	16.	A
7.	D	17.	C
8.	C	18.	C
9.	D	19.	B
10.	D	20.	D

EXAMINATION SECTION
TEST 1

DIRECTIONS: Each question or incomplete statement is followed by several suggested answers or completions. Select the one that BEST answers the question or completes the statement. *PRINT THE LETTER OF THE CORRECT ANSWER IN THE SPACE AT THE RIGHT.*

1. The informed editorial assistant knows that the difference between a copy reader and a proofreader is that the copy reader
    A. checks copy against type proofs
    B. checks galleys
    C. edits material submitted by writers
    D. holds copy for the proofreader

    1.____

2. *Style* to a copy editor means
    A. following a set pattern when rules of spelling and punctuation are equivocal
    B. following the rules of formal grammar
    C. making sure that the writing is not elegant
    D. making sure that the writing is polished

    2.____

3. An unbound copy of a book that has yet to be proofread is often called a
    A. galley proof
    B. copy draft
    C. folio
    D. pre-proof

    3.____

4. A tool in word-processing software that allows multiple users to make and accept revisions is known as
    A. spell check
    B. track changes
    C. cell merge
    D. simple revise

    4.____

5. One of the proofreader's primary responsibilities is to ensure that
    A. a magazine feature follows house style guidelines
    B. news sources have been properly vetted
    C. an article uses proper punctuation
    D. a story is concise while including all pertinent information

    5.____

6. According to standard editing protocol, to abbreviate the word *Company*, as in Jones Widget Company, a copy editor should
    A. circle the word
    B. cross out excess letters and put a period over the *m*
    C. cross out the entire word and write *Co.* above it in the space between the lines
    D. cross out the entire word and write *Co.* in margin, running a line to its position

    6.____

7. In editing copy, it is often necessary to indicate that numerals are to be spelled out. This is done by
   A. circling the numeral
   B. crossing out the numeral and spelling it out between the lines
   C. crossing out the numeral and spelling it out in margin with a line drawn to its position
   D. drawing a square around the numeral

8. Multi-user software that allows writers, editors and other editorial personnel to collaborate on documents in real time is known as a
   A. content management system
   B. collaborative management system
   C. digital publishing portal
   D. desktop publishing application

9. Type size is measured
   A. ems
   B. inches
   C. picas
   D. points

10. A pica measures approximately _____ and is typically used in _____.
    A. 1/6 of an inch; Microsoft Word
    B. 1/6 of an inch; Adobe InDesign
    C. 1/12 of an inch; Microsoft Excel
    D. 1/12 of an inch; QuarkXPress

11. Columns are measured in
    A. ems
    B. fractions of a page
    C. picas
    D. points

12. 36 points is
    A. about an inch
    B. about half an inch
    C. about two inches
    D. none of the foregoing

13. Which of the following is MOST relevant to news writers and editors?
    A. Chicago Manual of Style
    B. APA Publication Manual
    C. Associated Press Stylebook
    D. New York Times Manual of Style

14. The letters in italic type
    A. are less cursive than in roman type
    B. are more formal than in roman type
    C. are set by hand
    D. slant bottom left to top right

15. Sans-serif type
    A. has no additional fonts
    B. has no curlicues
    C. has no hangers or risers
    D. is old-fashioned German type

Questions 16-20.

DIRECTIONS: Questions 16 through 20 consist of groups of four words.
Select answer A if only ONE word is spelled correctly in a group.
Select answer B if TWO words are spelled correctly in a group,
Select answer C if THREE words are spelled correctly in a group.
Select answer D if all FOUR words are spelled correctly in a group.

16. counterfeit	embarass	panicky	supercede	16.____
17. benefited	personnel	questionnaire	unparalelled	17.____
18. bankruptcy	describable	proceed	vacuum	18.____
19. handicapped	mispell	offerred	pilgrimmage	19.____
20. corduroy	interfere	privilege	separator	20.____

Questions 21-25.

DIRECTIONS: For each question numbered 21 through 25, select the option whose meaning is MOST NEARLY the same as that of the numbered item.

21. CONDONE   21.____
    A. complete   B. condemn   C. cooperate   D. pardon

22. EXTENUATE   22.____
    A. accuse   B. excuse   C. lengthen   D. narrow

23. MORDANT   23.____
    A. caustic   B. depressed   C. dying   D. unwholesome

24. SPATE   24.____
    A. broad road   B. excessive quantity
    C. fish eggs   D. mineral springs

25. TORTUOUS   25.____
    A. devious   B. foul   C. injurious   D. painful

KEY (CORRECT ANSWERS)

1.	C		11.	C
2.	A		12.	B
3.	A		13.	C
4.	B		14.	D
5.	C		15.	B
6.	A		16.	B
7.	A		17.	C
8.	A		18.	D
9.	D		19.	A
10.	B		20.	D

21. D
22. B
23. A
24. B
25. A

TEST 2

DIRECTIONS: Each question or incomplete statement is followed by several suggested answers or completions. Select the one that BEST answers the question or completes the statement. *PRINT THE LETTER OF THE CORRECT ANSWER IN THE SPACE AT THE RIGHT.*

1. Of the following, the one that is NOT a main responsibility of a magazine or newspaper writer is
    A. writing the article's headline
    B. choosing the quotes to run in the story
    C. interviewing sources with relevant information
    D. writing for the intended audience

    1.____

2. Press releases received by a newspaper are usually directed to the
    A. city editor   B. managing editor
    C. promotion manager   D. publisher

    2.____

3. The agency of the United States Government that supervises radio and television broadcasting is known by the abbreviation
    A. ABC   B. FCC   C. FTC   D. SEC

    3.____

4. In a news article, the *nut graph* (or *graf*) is used
    A. to separate and highlight the most important quotes
    B. as a key visual element that enhances the story
    C. to detail the most pertinent information and why it is important
    D. to display the writer's contact information

    4.____

5. Of the following, the type of publicity MOST likely to promote morale of the employees of your department would be a(n)
    A. article concerning the department written for a technical publication
    B. article in the annual report summarizing the activities of the department
    C. local newspaper article on the accomplishments of the employees of the agency
    D. short blurb on your superior carried by the Associated Press

    5.____

6. If you wanted one photograph of a street accident to illustrate the need for improving traffic control at the scene of the accident, you should select a picture that shows
    A. a close-up of the cars and the victim
    B. a policeman questioning witnesses at the accident scene
    C. the cars and the victim against the whole intersection of the accident scene
    D. the victim being put into an ambulance

    6.____

7. The opening paragraph of a news article is known as the
    A. topic   B. subhead   C. leader   D. lede

    7.____

11

8. A copy editor assigned to work on a fiction novel is unsure if a particular phrase should be set in italics. To check if italics are appropriate, the editor should
   A. refer to the Chicago Manual of Style
   B. e-mail an excerpt to a fellow editor for guidance
   C. confer with the writer and come to an agreement on proper style
   D. refer to the Associated Press Stylebook

   8.____

9. In publishing software, *bleed* is a term related to
   A. graphic images
   B. run-on sentences
   C. red editing marks
   D. page layout

   9.____

10. A picture in a newspaper is accompanied by a description that reads:
    OLD MAN WINTER RETURNS
    Timmy Harris, 8, builds a snowman at Laramie Park on the first afternoon of winter.

    In newspaper parlance, the phrase "Old Man Winter Returns" is known as the
    A. headline   B. caption   C. cutline   D. subhead

    10.____

Questions 11-20.

DIRECTIONS: In Questions 11 through 20, print in the space at the right the capital letter immediately preceding the word or phrase which is CLOSEST in meaning to that of the capitalized letter.

11. BIBLIOPHILE
    A. appendix
    C. list of references
    B. library
    D. lover of books

    11.____

12. SACERDOTAL
    A. penitential   B. priestly   C. reminiscent   D. spiritual

    12.____

13. FLAGELLATE
    A. communicate by signals
    C. play the flute
    B. pillage
    D. scourge

    13.____

14. SAGA
    A. epoch   B. hero   C. inscription   D. legend

    14.____

15. APOCRYPHAL
    A. annotated   B. orthodox   C. unauthentic   D. visionary

    15.____

16. CAVIL
    A. make captious objection
    C. render just praise
    B. punish severely
    D. warn emphatically

    16.____

17. SUPERFLUOUS
    A. impressive
    C. unnecessary
    B. formidable
    D. increasing

    17.____

18. ACCORD
    A. deceit B. agreement C. tension D. comfort

19. RUE
    A. abandon B. despair C. repent D. stain

20. CAPRICIOUS
    A. impulsive
    B. intimidating
    C. captivating
    D. unwholesome

21. Of the following, the grammatically CORRECT sentence is:
    A. Neither the mayor nor the city clerk are willing to talk.
    B. Neither the mayor nor the city clerk is willing to talk.
    C. Neither the mayor or the city clerk are willing to talk.
    D. Neither the mayor or the city clerk is willing to talk.

22. Of the following, the grammatically CORRECT sentence is:
    A. Being that he is that kind of boy, cooperation cannot be expected.
    B. He interviewed people who he thought had something to say.
    C. Stop whomever enters the building regardless of rank or office held.
    D. Passing through the countryside, the scenery pleased us.

23. Of the following, the grammatically CORRECT sentence is:
    A. The childrens' shoes were in their closet.
    B. The children's shoes were in their closet.
    C. The childs' shoes were in their closest.
    D. The childs' shoes were in his closet.

24. Of the following, the grammatically INCORRECT sentence is:
    A. Dissatisfaction with the theoretical bases and practical workings of the general property tax has given rise to two movements of tax reform.
    B. Let the book lie on the table.
    C. Since the department is reducing its number of employees is not proof that they are not needed.
    D. Who do you think will be selected for the position?

25. Of the following, the grammatically INCORRECT sentence is:
    A. Application of the principles discovered during those experiments have been of great value to mankind.
    B. Every one of the editorial assistants proved his worth without exception.
    C. State regulation of morals aids in the protection of the family.
    D. Working when one is tired does not yield the best results.

KEY (CORRECT ANSWERS)

1. A
2. A
3. B
4. C
5. C

6. C
7. D
8. A
9. D
10. B

11. D
12. B
13. D
14. D
15. C

16. A
17. C
18. B
19. C
20. A

21. B
22. B
23. B
24. C
25. A

EXAMINATION SECTION
TEST 1

DIRECTIONS: Each question or incomplete statement is followed by several suggested answers or completions. Select the one that BEST answers the question or completes the statement. *PRINT THE LETTER OF THE CORRECT ANSWER IN THE SPACE AT THE RIGHT.*

1. The basic data-entry units that make up a spreadsheet are called
   A. boxes   B. cells   C. sheets   D. tabs

2. You are assigned the task of creating a brochure that includes descriptions and images of the seasonal amenities available to town residents. The best software to use to create this brochure is
   A. Microsoft PowerPoint   B. Adobe InDesign
   C. Google Drive   D. Adobe Acrobat

3. The term *duplex* refers to
   A. prints with more than two colors   B. tabloid-style newspapers
   C. double-spaced printing   D. two-sided printing

4. Copyright law should be considered when an editor is
   A. thinking of synonyms that would enhance a magazine piece
   B. searching for images to run in a blog post
   C. deciding whether or not to use an anonymous source
   D. all of the above

5. Libel and slander both relate to the spread of false information, but differ in that libelous statements are _____ and slanderous statements are _____.
   A. violent; threatening   B. in newspapers; on the internet
   C. written; spoken   D. spoken; written

6. The proofreading mark used to indicate that text or punctuation should be inserted in a particular place is called a(n)
   A. asterisk   B. pound sign   C. caret   D. slash

7. A social media assistant is told to put up a Facebook post the day before a youth video-game tournament at the local library. To best promote the tournament and generate excitement, the body of the post should read
   A. "It's Gamer Day Eve! Come on down tomorrow for a fun-filled day playing your favorite games!"
   B. "VIDEO GAMES TOMORROW! SEE YOU THERE!!!"
   C. "GAME...ON!!! First annual City Library Gamer Day Tourney begins in T-minus 24 hours! See you at 10 a.m.!"
   D. "Mayor Johnson wishes all participants in tomorrow's Gamer Day Tourney at City Library the best of luck, and new high scores for all!"

8. It is your job to post videos on Instagram of the day's leading news stories. Each post must include an excerpt from the news article, and a short headline should appear as a banner over the footage.
Which of the following headlines is correct in both style and grammar?
   A. TOWN COUNSEL APPROVES PERMIT FOR NEW DISTILLERY
   B. TOWN COUNSEL ISSUES PERMIT FOR LOCAL BREWERY
   C. TOWN COUNCIL APPROVED PERMIT FOR NEW DISTILLERY
   D. TOWN COUNCIL ISSUES PERMIT FOR NEW DISTILLERY

8._____

9. To assure credibility and avoid hostility, a public relations specialist MUST
   A. make certain the message is truthful, not evasive or exaggerated
   B. make sure the message contains some dire consequences, if ignored
   C. repeat the message often enough to that it cannot be ignored
   D. try to reach as many people and groups as possible

9._____

10. The public relations specialist MUST be prepared to assume that members of an audience
    A. may have developed attitudes toward proposals, whether favorable, neutral or unfavorable
    B. will be immediately hostile
    C. will consider any proposals with an open mind
    D. will invariably need an introduction to the subject

10._____

11. To a copy editor, *slug* means
    A. first sentence of a story
    B. identification of a story
    C. size of type in which a story is to be set
    D. the story needs punch or drive

11._____

12. You are assigned to write the photo cutline for a cover story about new local shops in the Sunday Business section. The photo shows the owner of a new coffeehouse brewing espresso as a customer waits at the register.
The cutline should include all of the following information EXCEPT the
    A. name of the owner   B. location of the coffeehouse
    C. name of the coffeehouse   D. name of the customer

12._____

13. When covering political events, a group of reporters might distribute quotes and relevant information to a larger contingent of journalists. These reporters are called
    A. political correspondents   B. news desk reporters
    C. distributing journalists   D. pool reporters

13._____

14. The lede is the MOST important part of a news story.
It should
    A. attract the reader
    B. give all the facts immediately
    C. start with the source of the story
    D. start with the time of the story

14._____

15. There are several acceptable ways of writing a news story. 15.____
It should USUALLY be written
   A. as facts become known, regardless of chronology
   B. chronologically
   C. in order of decreasing importance or interest
   D. so that details come at the end

16. A reporter assigned to cover a scheduled broadcast speech GENERALLY 16.____
   A. gets shorthand notes afterwards
   B. takes shorthand notes himself
   C. receives an advance copy
   D. writes his story from the radio or television broadcast

17. A reporter is told that an interview has been set up for him for the next day with 17.____
an authority on earthquakes. He is given the name and affiliation of the
authority and the location and time of the interview.
His NEXT step is to
   A. bring along a seismology expert to the interview
   B. do research on seismology and get biographical data on the interviewee
   C. try to arrange a luncheon date with the interviewee
   D. verify time and place of interview

18. When a story is worth handling on a continuing basis, even if no added news is 18.____
available, a writer will be asked to
   A. call the sources on deadline and make sure no facts are changed
   B. rearrange the story, putting other details in the lead
   C. shorten the story
   D. write a *second day* lead

19. There are almost as many techniques of interviewing as there are interviewers. 19.____
Of the following, the LEAST objectionable method is to
   A. ask if interviewee minds being quoted
   B. make occasional notes as important topics come up
   C. take notes unobtrusively
   D. take shorthand notes of every word

20. There are many differences between feature and news stories. 20.____
The single MOST important difference is that
   A. features are longer than news stories
   B. features emphasize the unusual; news stories the significant
   C. features ignore facts that news stories cannot
   D. news stories are more timely than features

Questions 21-25.

DIRECTIONS: In each of Questions 21 through 25, only one of the four sentences conforms to standards of correct usage. The other three contain errors in grammar, diction or punctuation. Select the option in each question which conforms to standards of correct usage. Consider an option correct if it contains none of the errors mentioned above, even though there may be other correct ways of expressing the same thought.

21. A. Because he was ill was no excuse for his behavior. 21.____
    B. I insist that he see a lawyer before he goes to trial.
    C. He said "that he had not intended to go."
    D. He wasn't out of the office only three days.

22. A. He came to the station and pays a porter to carry his bags into the train. 22.____
    B. I should have liked to live in medieval times.
    C. My father was born in Linville. A little country town where everyone knows everyone else.
    D. The car, which is parked across the street, is disabled.

23. A. He asked the desk clerk for a clean, quiet, room. 23.____
    B. I expected James to be lonesome and that he would want to go home.
    C. I have stopped worrying because I have heard nothing further on the subject.
    D. If the board of directors controls the company, they may take actions which are disapproved by the stockholders.

24. A. Each of the players knew their place. 24.____
    B. He whom you saw on the stage is the son of an actor.
    C. Susan is the smartest of the twin sisters.
    D. Who ever thought of him winning both prizes?

25. A. An outstanding trait of early man was their reliance on omens. 25.____
    B. Because I had never been there before.
    C. Neither Mr. Jones nor Mr. Smith has completed his work.
    D. While eating my dinner, a dog came to the window.

5 (#1)

KEY (CORRECT ANSWERS)

1.	B		11.	B
2.	B		12.	D
3.	D		13.	D
4.	B		14.	A
5.	C		15.	C
6.	C		16.	C
7.	C		17.	B
8.	D		18.	D
9.	A		19.	C
10.	A		20.	B

21. B
22. B
23. C
24. B
25. C

TEST 2

DIRECTIONS: Each question or incomplete statement is followed by several suggested answers or completions. Select the one that BEST answers the question or completes the statement. *PRINT THE LETTER OF THE CORRECT ANSWER IN THE SPACE AT THE RIGHT.*

1. In a pre-edited news article or press release, ____ indicates the end of text. 1.____
   A. -30-   B. -end-   C. stet   D. -XX-

2. The term *double truck* is used to describe 2.____
   A. a two-column headline
   B. the first page of the second section
   C. two adjacent pages made up as one
   D. two pictures combined into a single picture

3. To indicate that a correction should be ignored and text left as is, an editor should use the notation 3.____
   A. stet   B. as/is   C. -#-   D. check

4. As a copy editor, you are assigned to edit an article about the local high school football team's summer training camp. The lede of the article reads: 4.____
   "Practice makes perfect, and based on early showing at camp, Marlboro might be in line for its finest season in a decade."
   This article should be sent back to the writer for revisions because
   A. clichés should be avoided in news articles, especially in the lede
   B. technically it's not accurate that practice makes perfect
   C. few readers are familiar with the history of the team
   D. the opinion of the writer is not relevant in a news article

5. The terms *vector* and *PNG* refer to 5.____
   A. peripheral devices   B. the first word processors
   C. font packages   D. computer graphics

6. The technique of trimming a photo to be used in a news story is known as 6.____
   A. casting off   B. cropping   C. routing   D. scaling down

7. Which of the following fonts would be most suitable for use in the website version of a news article? 7.____
   A. Helvetica   B. Baskerville   C. Garamond   D. Comic Sans

8. If the same article from question #7 is to be read in the print edition of the newspaper, the most suitable serif font would be 8.____
   A. Arial   B. Times   C. Verdana   D. Copperplate

9. In typography, the number of points to an inch is APPROXIMATELY 9.____
   A. 12   B. 48   C. 72   D. 96

10. All variants of a particular type design are said to belong to the same 10.____
    A. family   B. font   C. quad   D. run

11. Old English is in a class of type known as
    A. black letter   B. italic   C. roman   D. script

12. Which of the following is a sans serif font?
    A. Baskerville   B. Bodoni   C. Verdana   D. Garamond

13. The one of the following that is NOT associated with typography is
    A. kerning   B. cropping   C. leading   D. tracking

14. Of the following, the term that is NOT associated with the printing process is
    A. collate   B. duplex   C. export   D. offset

15. A large capital letter used as block text at the start of a paragraph is called a
    A. letter block   B. drop cap   C. drophead   D. subhead

16. A method of printing in which a relief process is used is
    A. intaglio   B. letter press   C. lithography   D. offset

17. A screened engraving of a photograph is known as
    A. intaglio   B. letter press   C. lithography   D. offset

18. In typography, the term used for arranging type in lines so that all the lines in a column are even is
    A. conversion   B. furnishing   C. justifying   D. leading

19. The front page of THE NEW YORK TIMES most frequently exemplifies the make-up known as
    A. balanced
    B. circus
    C. focus
    D. hanging indentation

20. Information about a newspaper's publisher, offices and subscription rates are typically found
    A. on the editorial page
    B. in the masthead
    C. beneath the lead story
    D. in the classified section

21. The word *stet* tells the printer to
    A. capitalize all letters in the phrase
    B. omit the phrase
    C. reinstate the phrase marked out
    D. set the marked phrase in italics

22. In proofreading, the symbol ✓✓✓ indicates that the printer should
    A. check with original manuscript
    B. correct faulty spacing
    C. insert quotation marks
    D. straighten lines

23. A proofreader indicates a *bad or defective letter* by the symbol   23.____
    A. ✗   B. ▢   C. ∽   D. ♯

24. The proofreading symbol meaning *close up partly but leave some space* is   24.____
    A. (/)   B. ⊙   C. ♯̄   D. ▢

25. A proof containing the misspelling *Beleive* should be marked   25.____
    A. tr   B. wf   C. ⊙   D. ⌐

KEY (CORRECT ANSWERS)

1.	A	11.	A
2.	C	12.	C
3.	A	13.	B
4.	A	14.	C
5.	D	15.	B
6.	B	16.	B
7.	A	17.	A
8.	B	18.	C
9.	C	19.	A
10.	A	20.	B

21. C
22. B
23. A
24. C
25. A

GRAPHIC ARTS

EXAMINATION SECTION
TEST 1

DIRECTIONS: Each question or incomplete statement is followed by several suggested answers or completions. Select the one that BEST answers the question or completes the statement. *PRINT THE LETTER OF THE CORRECT ANSWER IN THE SPACE AT THE RIGHT.*

1. The term mitography is synonymous with _____ printing. 1.____
   A. relief
   B. lithographic
   C. screen
   D. intaglio

2. Photography is PRIMARILY used in _____ printing. 2.____
   A. planographic
   B. stencil
   C. relief
   D. silk screen

3. A good project for a beginning class in photography would be to make 3.____
   A. contact prints
   B. enlargements
   C. montages
   D. murals

4. A linoleum block is used to reproduce a 4.____
   A. dry point
   B. line drawing
   C. mezzotint
   D. aquatint

5. The process of preparing a press to obtain the proper printing impression is referred to as 5.____
   A. lock-up
   B. paste-up
   C. make-ready
   D. make-up

6. The vehicle used in the manufacture of printing ink is 6.____
   A. pigment
   B. varnish
   C. dryer
   D. alcohol

7. As an aid in accurately locating gauge pins on the platen press, the FIRST impression is always printed on 7.____
   A. a sheet of thin scrap paper
   B. a single sheet of bristol index
   C. the tympan sheet
   D. the proof press

8. A line on a dry point plate is made 8.____
   A. with a bruin
   B. by etching with acid
   C. with a linoleum gouge
   D. by scratching the surface with a needle

9. Lumarith is a material used to make a
   A. linoleum cut B. half-tone print
   C. dry point engraving D. metallic stamping

10. The guides MOST frequently used in silk screen printing are _____ guides.
    A. pin B. quad C. metal D. paper

11. Direct image plastiplates BEST serve to demonstrate _____ printing.
    A. relief B. intaglio
    C. planographic D. letterpress

12. In making a rubber stamp, the type impression is made
    A. on unvulcanized rubber B. on molding board
    C. on a mica base D. directly on the mount

13. Lithography is preferred in certain situations because
    A. it requires no make-ready
    B. oil and water do not mix
    C. it is a fast printing process
    D. various colored inks would be printed simultaneously

14. A doctor blade would be found on a
    A. rotogravure press B. letterpress
    C. offset press D. bookbinder's press

15. The wire stapler is used to make the _____ stitch.
    A. kettle B. smyth C. saddle D. in-and-out

16. Headband is BEST described as
    A. a decorative strip of cloth placed at both ends of a bound book
    B. the strip of cloth that helps strengthen the hinge of a book
    C. the outer binding
    D. the metallic stamped line

17. An edition bound book has a _____ cover.
    A. paper B. case C. plastic D. flexible

18. Of the following, the type that is classified as script is
    A. Century schoolbook B. Spartan
    C. Bernhard light D. Goudy oldstyle

19. The plan of work in typesetting is referred to as a
    A. copy fitting B. layout
    C. blue point D. working drawing

20. The paper BEST suited for the printing of a lunch ticket is _____ paper.
    A. bond B. antique C. index D. coated

21. A rubber stamp is an example of _____ printing. 21._____

    A. stencil B. relief
    C. planographic D. intaglio

22. In locking up a type form in the chase, the quoins are always placed 22._____

    A. above and below the form
    B. above and to the right of the form
    C. below and to the left of the form
    D. to the left and to the right of the form

23. Type forms are tied 23._____

    A. on the proof press B. on the bank
    C. in the chase D. in the galley

24. Capital letters are arranged alphabetically in the California Job case with the exception of the letters 24._____

    A. *E* and *O* B. *J* and *U* C. *J* and *T* D. *T* and *U*

25. A line of type 3 1/2" in length is equal to _____ picas. 25._____

    A. 11 B. 15 C. 19 D. 21

KEY (CORRECT ANSWERS)

1.	C	11.	C
2.	A	12.	B
3.	A	13.	C
4.	B	14.	A
5.	C	15.	C
6.	B	16.	A
7.	C	17.	B
8.	D	18.	C
9.	C	19.	B
10.	D	20.	C

21. B
22. B
23. D
24. B
25. D

TEST 2

DIRECTIONS: Each question or incomplete statement is followed by several suggested answers or completions. Select the one that BEST answers the question or completes the statement. *PRINT THE LETTER OF THE CORRECT ANSWER IN THE SPACE AT THE RIGHT.*

1. If 10 point 3-em quads are not available, the spaces that can be used from the 30-point case are

    A. 5-em spaces
    B. 4-em spaces
    C. 3-em spaces
    D. em-quads

    1.___

2. Of the following, the type face that is classified as modern is

    A. Bodoni   B. Cloister   C. Garamond   D. Cheltenham

    2.___

3. In setting gauge pins for a 3" x 5" card, the MOST suitable arrangement of the pins is

    A. one to the left, bottom and right
    B. two to the left, bottom and right
    C. two to the left and one on the bottom
    D. one to the left and two on the bottom

    3.___

4. In printing a business card, the form is placed in the chase with the head to the

    A. left   B. bottom   C. right   D. top

    4.___

5. The principle of the lithographic printing process may be demonstrated by using _____ plates.

    A. direct image plasti-
    B. washoff
    C. zinc
    D. dycrill

    5.___

6. In silk screen printing, a frisket is used

    A. for centering the film on the frame
    B. to speed up the printing process
    C. to keep the job clean
    D. to help in feeding the job

    6.___

7. In making rubber stamps, mica powder is used

    A. on the vulcanizing rubber
    B. to polish the press
    C. on the molding board
    D. to prepare the stamp for mounting

    7.___

8. In silk screen printing, register is obtained by

    A. pin guides
    B. quad guides
    C. thumb tacks
    D. paper guides

    8.___

9. Photographic enlarging paper is known as _____ paper.

    A. bromide   B. chloride   C. halide   D. fluoride

    9.___

26

10. In bookbinding, a signature is the

   A. name of the publisher
   B. author's name
   C. folded section of a book
   D. final *OK* from the customer

11. A linoleum block is a _____ printing plate.

   A. relief
   B. lithographic
   C. incised
   D. stereotype

12. A plate mark is characteristic of a print made by

   A. mitography
   B. a dry-point etching
   C. photogravure
   D. flexography

13. A hard binding should be used on a book that is

   A. edition bound
   B. hand sewn
   C. wide-wire stitched
   D. plastic bound

14. The number of 17" x 22" paper sheets needed to make 1000 pieces of 8 1/2" x 11" paper is

   A. 175   B. 200   C. 250   D. 325

15. In locking a heavy form for the platen press, the form is positioned

   A. below the center of the chase
   B. according to the grippers on the press
   C. in any position sideways of the chase
   D. against the bottom of the chase

16. Proofreader's marks placed in a circle indicate the omission of a

   A. hyphen   B. apostrophe   C. comma   D. period

17. Of the following, the process that is NOT used to make printing plates is _____ plate.

   A. halftone
   B. stereotype
   C. zinc
   D. lithographic

18. A line of type 4 1/2" in length will measure _____ picas.

   A. 25   B. 26   C. 27   D. 28

19. Plate oil mixed with ink is used for

   A. silk screen printing
   B. lithographic printing
   C. flexographic printing
   D. printing an etching

20. Photographic contact prints are made by using a(n)

   A. printing frame
   B. enlarger
   C. vacuum frame
   D. type frame

21. Transtrace is a material used to make

   A. linoleum blocks
   B. silk screen stencils
   C. rubber stamps
   D. lithographic prints

22. The basis size of book paper is
    A. 25" x 38"
    B. 17" x 22"
    C. 22 1/2" x 28 1/2"
    D. 20" x 36"

23. The CORRECT size of professional stationery is
    A. 5 1/2" x 8 1/2"   B. 7 1/2" x 10 1/4"   C. 8 1/2" x 11"   D. 9" x 12"

24. Imposition refers to the placing of pages
    A. in the center of the chase
    B. allowing for the correct margins
    C. additional author corrections on page
    D. in correct order for folding

25. Antique finish paper is used extensively for the printing of
    A. books   B. letterheads   C. halftones   D. linecuts

KEY (CORRECT ANSWERS)

1.	C	11.	A
2.	A	12.	B
3.	D	13.	A
4.	B	14.	C
5.	A	15.	A
6.	C	16.	D
7.	A	17.	B
8.	D	18.	C
9.	A	19.	D
10.	C	20.	A

21. D
22. A
23. B
24. D
25. A

TEST 3

DIRECTIONS: Each question or incomplete statement is followed by several suggested answers or completions. Select the one that BEST answers the question or completes the statement. *PRINT THE LETTER OF THE CORRECT ANSWER IN THE SPACE AT THE RIGHT.*

1. The manufacturer's basic size for bond paper is　　　　　　　　　　　　　　　　1.____
   A. 8 1/2" x 11"　　B. 17" x 22"　　C. 25" x 38"　　D. 32" x 44"

2. Of the following names, the one that does NOT refer to the finish on paper is　　2.____
   A. eggshell　　B. antique　　C. english　　D. bond

3. The word *signature* refers to　　　　　　　　　　　　　　　　　　　　　　　　3.____
   A. offset printing　　　　　　　B. dry point etching
   C. book binding　　　　　　　　D. silk screen printing

4. The heavy starched cloth used for reinforcing the back of a book is called　　　4.____
   A. binder's cloth　　　　　　　B. super
   C. book cloth　　　　　　　　　D. buckram

5. Of the following, the one that is NOT a basic method of printing is　　　　　　5.____
   A. relief　　B. offset　　C. gravure　　D. silkscreen

6. The consistency of silk screen *ink* is similar to that of　　　　　　　　　　　6.____
   A. water　　　　　　　　　　　B. paint
   C. letterpress ink　　　　　　　D. job ink

7. Of the following, the one that is NOT a form of imitation engraving is　　　　7.____
   A. lithography　　　　　　　　B. process embossing
   C. thermography　　　　　　　D. virkotyping

8. Of the following, the one that is a part of a printing press is　　　　　　　　8.____
   A. guides　　B. packing　　C. platen　　D. tympan

9. To miss an impression during a run on a platen press, one uses the　　　　　9.____
   A. grippers　　　　　　　　　　B. throw-off lever
   C. chase　　　　　　　　　　　D. foot treadle

10. The name *Nu-film* is related to　　　　　　　　　　　　　　　　　　　　　10.____
    A. gravure　　　　　　　　　　B. letterpress
    C. offset　　　　　　　　　　　D. silk screen

11. The spacer MOST commonly used between words when setting type is　　　11.____
    A. em quad　　B. 3-em space　　C. en quad　　D. 5-em space

12. To be sure a type is positioned properly in composition, one must check the　12.____
    A. feet　　B. face　　C. serifs　　D. nicks

13. Of the following letters, the one that is NOT a *type demon* is

    A. b   B. p   C. e   D. q

14. There are 12 points in one

    A. pica   B. inch   C. nonpareil   D. lead

15. All of the following are used when locking up a form EXCEPT

    A. guides   B. quoins   C. furniture   D. chase

16. In taking proofs on a proof press, the form is held in a

    A. stick   B. case   C. galley   D. rack

17. Adjusting the impression of a printing run can BEST be accomplished by

    A. make-ready
    B. moving the grippers
    C. tightening the guides
    D. adjusting the platen

18. Three-color reproduction of pictures requires the use of all of the following colors EXCEPT

    A. red   B. black   C. yellow   D. blue

19. The word *slug* commonly refers to a line space of _____ points.

    A. 4   B. 2   C. 6   D. 8

20. The word *lead* commonly refers to a line space of _____ point(s).

    A. 1   B. 2   C. 3   D. 4

21. A matrix would be found on all of the following machines EXCEPT the

    A. linotype
    B. Ludlow
    C. intertype
    D. photocompositor

22. Of the following, the screen cut producing the CLEAREST picture would be

    A. 150   B. 100   C. 130   D. 60

23. To reproduce a photograph using the letterpress printing method, the printer would need a

    A. line cut
    B. halftone
    C. line engraving
    D. stereotype

24. Of the following, the one that is NOT used in locking up a form is the

    A. chase   B. furniture   C. quoins   D. tympan

25. Cold-type composition is related MOST closely to _____ printing.

    A. relief   B. offset   C. italio   D. silkscreen

KEY (CORRECT ANSWERS)

1. B
2. D
3. C
4. B
5. D

6. B
7. A
8. C
9. B
10. D

11. B
12. D
13. C
14. A
15. A

16. C
17. A
18. B
19. C
20. B

21. D
22. A
23. B
24. D
25. B

TEST 4

DIRECTIONS: Each question or incomplete statement is followed by several suggested answers or completions. Select the one that BEST answers the question or completes the statement. *PRINT THE LETTER OF THE CORRECT ANSWER IN THE SPACE AT THE RIGHT.*

1. The term *side face* is used to describe one kind of

    A. bookbinding B. rule
    C. silk screen stencil D. chase

2. *Nu-film* is used in

    A. the silk screen process
    B. the Ozalid Dyphoto process
    C. the Land direct print process
    D. making offset press negatives

3. Hypo is used as a

    A. developer B. stop bath
    C. wetting agent D. fixer

4. *Work and twist* is a term used to describe a technique in

    A. printing columnar jobs
    B. printing on both sides of a sheet
    C. doping inks
    D. making certain hand-made paper

5. An example of a kerned letter is

    A. f B. z C. m D. a

6. Bond inks are BEST suited for printing on

    A. rough uncoated wood fiber paper
    B. coated and enameled book stock
    C. cover stock
    D. ledger paper

7. The BEST place to add ink on the inking disc during a run on a platen press is on the _____ side.

    A. upper left B. upper right
    C. lower right D. lower left

8. The proofreader's mark *Sp. out* means

    A. remove the space
    B. space out - increase the spacing
    C. delete
    D. spell out

2 (#4)

9. The Fourdrinier machine is used in the process of   9._____
   A. gravure printing B. intaglio printing
   C. paper making D. Tusche printing

10. Compared to *winter* rollers, *summer* ink rollers contain   10._____
    A. more glue B. less rubber
    C. more softening materials D. less glue

11. A 3-em space of 12 point type is _____ points wide.   11._____
    A. 2 B. 3 C. 4 D. 5

12. The number of 5-em spaces needed to equal a 3-em quad is   12._____
    A. 1 2/3 B. 6 C. 8 D. 15

13. Swash characters are   13._____
    A. a variation of Roman types
    B. similar to cursives
    C. special forms of some text fonts
    D. made in upper case only

14. The number of 28" x 38" sheets required for 2000 programs, 6" x 9", with a 5% allowance for spoilage, is   14._____
    A. 63 B. 66 C. 118 D. 263

15. An aniline-dye carbon paper is used in printing.   15._____
    A. offset B. silk screen
    C. mimeograph D. spirit duplicator

16. A paste-up can be reproduced on a mimeograph stencil by a   16._____
    A. scan-o-graver B. stenafax
    C. spirit duplicator D. visual duplicator

17. FREEDOM OF THE PRESS is associated with the early American printer,   17._____
    A. William Bradford B. Benjamin Franklin
    C. Stephen Daye D. John Zenger

18. A duplicate of a type form used on a letterpress is known as a(n)   18._____
    A. electrotype B. zinc plate
    C. halftone plate D. offset plate

19. If the background of a dry point etching is too dark, the cause is PROBABLY   19._____
    A. too much ink B. too much roller pressure
    C. inadequate wiping D. inadequate paper conditioning

20. In setting gauge pins on a printing press for a 3" x 5" card, the gauge pins should be placed in the following positions: 20._____
    A. One each to the left, bottom and right
    B. Two each to the left, bottom and right

C. One to the left and two at the bottom
D. Two to the left and one at the bottom

21. The inside sheets of a photo album are held together with
    A. glue
    B. wire stitches
    C. kettle stitches
    D. lacing

22. A hard binding should be used on a book that is
    A. side-wire stitched
    B. hand-sewn
    C. edition bound
    D. plastic bound

23. In printing a business card, the form is placed in the chase with the head to the
    A. left
    B. bottom
    C. right
    D. top

24. In silk screen printing, tusche is used in making a _____ stencil.
    A. paper
    B. washout
    C. film
    D. photographic

25. In silk screen printing, a frisket is used to
    A. center the film on the frame
    B. speed up the printing process
    C. keep the job clean
    D. help feed the job

KEY (CORRECT ANSWERS)

1.	B		11.	C
2.	A		12.	D
3.	D		13.	B
4.	A		14.	C
5.	A		15.	D
6.	D		16.	B
7.	D		17.	D
8.	D		18.	A
9.	C		19.	C
10.	A		20.	C

21. D
22. C
23. B
24. B
25. C

EXAMINATION SECTION
TEST 1

DIRECTIONS: Each question or incomplete statement is followed by several suggested answers or completions. Select the one that BEST answers the question or completes the statement. *PRINT THE LETTER OF THE CORRECT ANSWER IN THE SPACE AT THE RIGHT.*

1. Which of the following is a nonsilver coating for photographic contact printing? 1.____

    A. Intaglio   B. Mezzotint   C. Cicero   D. Diazo

2. According to the *sequence* principle in design, the eye usually travels in each of the following ways when viewing a printed page EXCEPT from 2.____

    A. the upper-left corner to the lower-right
    B. big to small
    C. black to color
    D. bold to light

3. If any part of the image area on the plate deteriorates during the printing process, _____ has occurred. 3.____

    A. slurring   B. warp
    C. calendering   D. walk-off

4. Kneaded rubber erasers are most appropriate for use with 4.____

    A. chalks and charcoals   B. pencil
    C. drawing ink   D. dirt

5. In printing, any copy suitable for reproduction without using a halftone screen is referred to as _____ copy. 5.____

    A. hot   B. wireframe   C. line   D. hard

6. Which of the following steps in preparing a mechanical is typically performed LAST? 6.____

    A. Marking bleed lines   B. Pasting down type and art
    C. Marking key lines   D. Preparing an overlay

7. Which of the following is a typical bit depth for grayscale images in computer applications? 7.____

    A. 1   B. 8   C. 14   D. 24

8. Which of the following characteristics of color is used to describe lightness or darkness? 8.____

    A. Chroma   B. Saturation
    C. Hue   D. Value

9. A general rule in design is that if reverse print is used, it should not be set in type smaller than _____ points, in order to be readable. 9.____

    A. 10   B. 12   C. 14   D. 18

10. In print technology, the simulation of tones by using dot patterns of varying intensity is known as

    A. halftoning
    C. grayscaling
    B. stippling
    D. pixellation

11. Which of the following is NOT a rule of thumb for the capitalization of headlines during mechanical preparation?

    A. Capitalize any word with four or more letters.
    B. The most readable headlines are written in all caps.
    C. As an infinitive, *To* is always capitalized, but not as a preposition.
    D. Any word that starts a line should be capitalized, even if it is in the middle of the headline.

12. In CAD/CAM applications, what is the term for the feature which tells the user where he or she is in terms of the x, y, or z coordinates?

    A. Coordinate tracking
    C. User-defined views
    B. Virtual reality
    D. Auto-dimensioning

13. Which of the following is the most appropriate use for hot-press illustration board?

    A. Layouts
    C. Transferring sketches
    B. First roughs
    D. Mechanicals

14. Which of the following processes is involved in the preparation of a *flat* for offset printing plate exposure?

    A. Keylining   B. Trapping   C. Stripping   D. Markup

15. In typography, how many points make up a pica?

    A. 6   B. 9   C. 12   D. 18

16. Each of the following is a common benefit associated with the use of a mechanical in the preparation of artwork for press EXCEPT it

    A. saves time
    B. assures proper positioning of images on the page
    C. keeps type and line art elements intact as one unit
    D. allows proofing of in-place elements at a stage in production where changes are inexpensive

17. During color separation, a blue filter

    A. reflects yellow and cyan onto film
    B. absorbs all colors to create a black printer
    C. leaves nearly transparent areas in the cyan portions of the image
    D. leaves nearly transparent areas in the yellow portions of the image

18. Digital printing is fostering several essentially new printing markets that have not been prevalent in the past due to the cost of prepress and printing by conventional methods. Which of the following is NOT one of these markets?

    _____ printing.

    A. On-demand
    C. Short-run process
    B. Batch-processed
    D. Variable information

19. Each of the following statements about artist's drawing ink is true EXCEPT they

    A. are an excellent medium for line drawing
    B. are not transparent
    C. have good adhesion properties
    D. are waterproof

20. To offset the different ink layers in conventional process color separations, halftone screens for black should be placed at a _____° angle to one another to avoid undesirable moire patterns.

    A. 45   B. 75   C. 90   D. 105

21. Letterpress

    A. runs tend to be inconsistent
    B. does not have good halftone detail
    C. offers excellent tints
    D. is especially suited to textured paper

22. The LEAST expensive printing surfaces available today are

    A. intaglio plates   B. thermal serial heads
    C. lithographic plates   D. gravure rollers

23. Orange or red transparent masking film is typically used to

    A. define the trim marks on a mechanical
    B. define an area to be screened or tinted
    C. define a knockout
    D. prevent bleeding during the printing process

24. Each of the following is a component of the Agfa Chroma-press system for color printing EXCEPT

    A. RIP or raster image processor
    B. job entry subsystem
    C. output print engine
    D. server software

25. During paste-up, windows for halftones that are intended to bleed into the margin should be _____ in. beyond the trin line.

    A. 1/16 to 1/8   B. 1/8 to 1/4
    C. 1/4 to 1/2   D. 1/2 to 1

KEY (CORRECT ANSWERS)

1. D
2. C
3. D
4. A
5. C

6. D
7. B
8. D
9. A
10. A

11. B
12. A
13. D
14. C
15. C

16. A
17. D
18. B
19. B
20. A

21. C
22. C
23. B
24. B
25. B

———

TEST 2

DIRECTIONS: Each question or incomplete statement is followed by several suggested answers or completions. Select the one that BEST answers the question or completes the statement. *PRINT THE LETTER OF THE CORRECT ANSWER IN THE SPACE AT THE RIGHT.*

1. To secure all elements in place during the preparation of a mechanical, each of the following tools may be used EXCEPT   1.____

   A. a burnishing roller
   B. opaquing liquid
   C. smooth ivory stick
   D. a burnishing stick

2. Adjustable triangles used in design work should at the very least be _____ inches long on one side.   2.____

   A. 6   B. 8   C. 10   D. 14

3. The flat or rolled surface against which paper is held during the printing process is generally known as the   3.____

   A. raster
   B. litho plate
   C. platen
   D. blanket cylinder

4. Which of the following is an *oldstyle* typeface?   4.____

   A. Folio   B. Times   C. Helvetica   D. Garamond

5. During the preparation of a mechanical, the image area should be positioned so that at LEAST a _____-inch margin exists outside of it for the placement of registration and other marks.   5.____

   A. $\frac{1}{2}$ B. 1   C. $1\frac{1}{2}$ D. 2

6. During color separation, an artist might prepare copy by outlining certain areas of the artwork on a tissue overlay, with instructions to the printer or camera operator. This is a process known as   6.____

   A. cropping   B. keylining   C. stripping   D. keystoning

7. Which of the following is a common use for a torchon in artwork?   7.____

   A. Bisecting a drawn line
   B. Achieving a fine point on a drawing pencil
   C. Masking off areas on the drawing surface
   D. Blending charcoal particles on the drawing surface

8. Which of the following is a form of proof from stripped film flats that is made before final plates are burned, in order to ensure correct pagination and location of illustrations and photos?   8.____

   A. Brownout
   B. Master proof
   C. Blueline
   D. Color proof

9. When working with a photograph during paste-up, an artist finds that the image is gray and flat in overall appearance. Which of the following is the best solution for improving a reprint?

    A. Use the burning-in technique
    B. Use the dodging technique
    C. Reproduce the shot as small as possible
    D. Trying a duller finish on the print

9._____

10. _____ is the prepress technique which allows for slight variations in registration during the press run.

    A. Trapping   B. Dithering
    C. Antialiasing   D. Stripping

10._____

11. Usually, holding lines on a mechanical are drawn in

    A. nonrepro blue pencil
    B. red ink with a ruling or technical pen
    C. cobalt blue ink with a ruling or technical pen
    D. black with a ruling or technical pen

11._____

12. When the action of light through positives produces a light-hardened coating on the non-image areas of lithographic printing plates, the plates are described as

    A. lossy   B. negative   C. halftoned   D. deep-etched

12._____

13. In computer graphics, a curve calculated by a mathematical function that connects separate points with a high degree of smoothness is known specifically as a(n)

    A. sine   B. Bezier   C. rollout   D. spline

13._____

14. What is the term for a line that extends from the outside edge of an object being dimensioned out to where the dimension text is printed?

    A. Witness line   B. Frontis
    C. Vector   D. Wireframe

14._____

15. In composing thumbnails, an artist should be concerned with each of the following EXCEPT

    A. shade   B. proportion
    C. weight   D. scale

15._____

16. Which of the following is a type of optical device used in the art studio to project enlarged or reduced images for tracing?

    A. Histogram   B. Lucey   C. Extruder   D. Overset

16._____

17. Which of the following brush types include short, curved-in, flat brushes?

    A. Flats   B. Brights   C. Fans   D. Sky

17._____

18. Which of the following is LEAST likely to be a problem associated with electrophotographic printing?

    A. There may be variations in batches of toners with identical formulations.
    B. There is currently no means of smoothing bitmapped screen fonts or images during printing.
    C. Volatile organic compounds used in liquid toner systems are subject to environmental regulations.
    D. Image density and tone reproduction may suffer as a result of charge voltage decay.

19. An item of artwork is to be reduced on a mechanical so that its width of 40 picas becomes a finished width of 10 picas. Assuming that the reduction is proportional, what percentage reduction will be necessary to achieve the finished width?

    A. 25   B. 33   C. 75   D. 400

20. Which of the following shading techniques in image processing renders facets of a polygon model as a single color based on their orientation to light and the viewer?

    A. Phong   B. Gouraud   C. Smooth   D. Flat

21. Which of the following is most suitable for transferring sketches to final art?

    A. Hot-press illustration board
    B. Bond paper
    C. Multi-media vellum
    D. Kid-finish bristol

22. What is the term for a calculation that determines how much space copy will take up when it is typeset?

    A. Assembly   B. Pulse   C. Spike   D. Castoff

23. When inking in stencils during layouts, the pen should generally be held at a _____° angle to the paper in order to ensure accuracy.

    A. 45   B. 60   C. 75   D. 90

24. To avoid trapping in a print job, one can create colors by overprinting, but in order for this to work there must be at LEAST _____% commonality in the colors placed adjacent to each other.

    A. 10   B. 20   C. 35   D. 50

25. In page printing, the folded sets of pages produced are known as

    A. signatures   B. impositions
    C. scores   D. flats

KEY (CORRECT ANSWERS)

1.	B	11.	B
2.	C	12.	D
3.	C	13.	D
4.	D	14.	A
5.	B	15.	C
6.	B	16.	B
7.	D	17.	B
8.	C	18.	B
9.	D	19.	C
10.	A	20.	D

21. C
22. D
23. D
24. B
25. A

EXAMINATION SECTION
TEST 1

DIRECTIONS: Each question or incomplete statement is followed by several suggested answers or completions. Select the one that BEST answers the question or completes the statement. *PRINT THE LETTER OF THE CORRECT ANSWER IN THE SPACE AT THE RIGHT.*

1. Which of the following is a type of color proof that represents the process combinations to be printed from four-color film?

    A. Pantone   B. Color Key   C. Lucey   D. Chromalin

2. In digital printing, _____ is the term used to denote pronounceable delineations between color and shading gradations.

    A. aliasing   B. banding   C. lapping   D. feathering

3. What is the term for the type of layout that features a single large illustration that dominates the space?

    A. Omnibus   B. Silhouette
    C. Picture window   D. Knockout

4. Which of the following characters has a unit count of 1½?

    A. L   B. ?   C. F   D. Y

5. The main difference between constructing a halftone window and making a screen or tint is that

    A. a screen is attached at the top with masking tape
    B. the window is on an overlay
    C. a screen can be supplied by the printer at the time press plates are made
    D. the window is on the basic artwork

6. To avoid *banding* in a scanned color image, an artist should have enough steps in the blend so that the length of each step is _____ points or less.

    A. 2   B. 4   C. 6   D. 8

7. Which of the following is used as a masking film to cover large image areas on mechanicals?

    A. Clear acetate   B. Prepared acetate
    C. Amberlith   D. Rubylith

8. Which of the following is NOT a disadvantage associated with the use of drum-based imagesetters for printing?

    A. Waste of film and time   B. Limited imaging area
    C. Low-quality output   D. High cost

9. Which of the following is a serif typeface?

    A. Myriad   B. Avant Garde
    C. Century Schoolbook   D. Helvetica

10. Rather than photographing each piece of art or photography separately for shooting negatives, they can be grouped together in a process known as

   A. clumping   B. clogging   C. chaining   D. ganging

11. If *FPO* is found written on a mechanical, it means that

   A. the proofreader has examined and approved the original copy
   B. there has been an error made by the printer or the typesetter
   C. the color on a prepress proof needs to be corrected
   D. the sized copy of a photograph or illustration is not to be used as camera-ready art

12. In which of the following types of presses are white highlights impossible?

   A. Flexography   B. Duplicate offset
   C. Screen   D. Xerography

13. During the printing process, which of the following is placed in direct contact with film in order to screen halftones?

   A. Line screen   B. Platen
   C. Splitter   D. Contact screen

14. Which of the following drawing media is most likely to produce a muddy, overworked effect in artwork?

   A. Fabricated chalk   B. Oil pastel
   C. Crayon   D. Charcoal

15. During the preparation of a mechanical, which of the following is the easiest way to lengthen copy that has already been set?

   A. Cutting text apart between paragraphs and adding more space
   B. Allowing more space between letters
   C. Setting paragraphs fully flush to the margins
   D. Add leading between lines

16. Printing paper that measures 20" x 25" is referred to specifically as

   A. board   B. bond   C. rule   D. royal

17. Which of the following is a possible DISADVANTAGE associated with the use of fm screening applications over halftone screening for the reproduction of tones in an image?

   A. Greater necessity for overprinting
   B. Lower ink densities reduce tonal range and contrast
   C. Ratio of white area to inked area changes can alter transfer curve calculations
   D. Larger printing dots create lower image detail

18. When a printed image is described as *low key*, it means it

   A. does not use halftones
   B. appears on the bottom half of the page
   C. takes up less than 1/4 of the page or surface
   D. is composed primarily of dark tones

19. On a printing press, the rubber-covered cylinders that transfer ink from the fountain onto the ink drum are known as the

   A. jack rollers
   B. distributing rollers
   C. impression cylinders
   D. blanket cylinders

19.____

20. During paste-up of copy, the rule of thumb is to typeset at least _____ to correct a single word or letter, so that the correction can be aligned properly.

   A. three words of type
   B. one line of type
   C. two lines of type
   D. the entire paragraph

20.____

21. What is the term for a printing press that prints both sides of the paper at one pass through the machine?

   A. Perfector   B. Pointer   C. Slug   D. Web press

21.____

22. When using colored pastels for artwork, a solution of _____, worked in with a small brush, can help to spread the color evenly over the surface.

   A. water
   B. washing soda
   C. paint thinner
   D. white gouache

22.____

23. Which of the following is a term for the degree to which a paper changes shape as a result of a change in atmospheric relative humidity?

   A. Distortion
   B. Expansivity
   C. Elongation
   D. Rigidity

23.____

24. An advantage of a duotone design over a duograph is that it

   A. counts as two colors for budgeting and scheduling purposes
   B. adds a second color by using an area of light color
   C. retains shadows and highlights
   D. uses only one negative

24.____

25. Which of the following is typically drawn first in the preparation of a mechanical?

   A. Bleed lines
   B. Crop marks
   C. Fold lines
   D. Outline

25.____

KEY (CORRECT ANSWERS)

1. D
2. B
3. C
4. D
5. D

6. A
7. C
8. C
9. C
10. D

11. D
12. A
13. D
14. B
15. A

16. D
17. C
18. D
19. B
20. C

21. A
22. C
23. B
24. C
25. D

———

TEST 2

DIRECTIONS: Each question or incomplete statement is followed by several suggested answers or completions. Select the one that BEST answers the question or completes the statement. *PRINT THE LETTER OF THE CORRECT ANSWER IN THE SPACE AT THE RIGHT.*

1. When ruling paste-up sheets that include camera-ready artwork for printing, vertical center lines and top trim lines should be drawn in
   I. pencil
   II. black ink
   III. nonrepro blue ink
   The CORRECT answer is:

   A. I *only* B. II *only* C. I or III D. I, II, or III

2. The process of reducing the size of a knockout when colors overlap one another is known as

   A. choking B. chopping
   C. cropping D. chromaticizing

3. Which of the following is most suitable for making carbon and photocopies?

   A. Fine line marker B. Technical pen
   C. Mechanical pencil D. Rolling writer

4. In lithographic press work, *hickeys* are likely to be caused by each of the following EXCEPT

   A. dry, hard particles on the printing plate or blanket
   B. hardened specks of ink
   C. an out-of-round transfer roller
   D. dirt on the press

5. Which of the following groups of typefaces makes use of the most radical *thick/thin* transition?

   A. Sans serif B. Modern
   C. Slab serif D. Oldstyle

6. Whenever an overlay is to be used during paste-up without pin registration, at least _____ transfer registration marks should be used on at least two sides of the basic artwork for alignment with corresponding marks on the overlay?

   A. 2 B. 3 C. 5 D. 6

7. Which of the following is/are advantages of indirect color separation over direct color separation?
   I. Faster and more efficient
   II. Greater control over color quality of the final negatives
   III. Allows for making different-sized separations from the intermediate steps without having to repeat the first part of the process
   The CORRECT answer is:

   A. I *only* B. I, II C. II, III D. III *only*

8. Which element of an electrophotographic imaging system is used to clean the photoconductor of the image just printed?

   A. Corona
   B. Photoreceptor belt
   C. Drum
   D. Solvent

9. Each of the following means the same as *degeneration* when working with art EXCEPT

   A. tone line conversion
   B. linear definition
   C. posterization
   D. two-tone posterization

10. In process-color reproduction, the process of masking is used primarily to

    A. select a portion of an image by cutting away parts from its edges
    B. electronically capture a single picture element
    C. reduce the size of a knockout when colors overlap
    D. reduce the contrast of transmitted light

11. In typography, how many picas make up an inch of type?

    A. 6　　B. 10　　C. 12　　D. 14

12. In computer graphics, what is the term for a visible defect in an image that is typically caused by limitations in the input or output processes?

    A. Artifact　　B. Spike　　C. Bit error　　D. Alias

13. Which of the following types or proofs are made of photosensitive paper that has been exposed with plate negatives?

    A. Pre-press proofs
    B. Press proofs
    C. Progressive proofs
    D. Blues

14. Which of the following progressive color proofs would be presented FIRST before the production run?

    A. Blue plate alone
    B. Black alone
    C. Yellow alone
    D. Yellow, red, and blue

15. In design, *balance* describes a state of equilibrium in which visual forces of equal strength pull in opposite directions. Which of the following is not a type of balance used in design work?

    A. Symmetrical
    B. Asymmetrical
    C. Centrifugal
    D. Radial

16. Which of the following is a printing method in which the image area is etched below the surface of the printing plate?

    A. Diazo
    B. Lithography
    C. Gravure
    D. Flexography

17. When an area of a photograph is too dark to reproduce well, the process of _____ may lighten it.

    A. dodging
    B. vignetting
    C. burning-in
    D. time exposure

18. A ream of paper in a print shop is labeled as *extensible.* This means that the paper

    A. can expand and contract with humidity and still hold an image
    B. is only to be used for electrostatic printing
    C. will withstand a sudden shock without tearing
    D. can be printed on both sides

19. Which of the following is LEAST likely to be a cause of press misregistration during the printing process?

    A. Plate misalignment
    B. Changes in humidity
    C. Changes in temperature
    D. High-speed paper handling

20. Which of the following is considered good design practice in typography?

    A. Choose a typeface that is short and thick to offset a tall and slender typeface
    B. Use a script and an italic on the same page
    C. Add importance to one element by making it bolder, and to another on the same page by making it bigger
    D. Using two scripts on the same page

21. Which of the following is an abbreviation for the chemical used to remove undeveloped silver from the emulsion of photographic film?

    A. Repro   B. Chroma   C. Hypo   D. Lucey

22. When ruling dummy sheets for a mechanical, which of the following may be ruled in picas, rather than inches or centimeters?

    A. Art measures   B. Gutters
    C. Spaces between columns   D. Margins

23. Photostats that are line converted are known as

    A. veloxes   B. luceys
    C. master stats D. halftones

24. In CAD/CAM applications, users can determine the physical characteristics of a given object by making use of a feature known as

    A. auto-dimensioning   B. solids modeling
    C. layering   D. user-defined views

25. Which of the following devices is used to determine correct photographic exposure for consistency on press?

    A. Lucey   B. Halftone screen
    C. Densitometer   D. Equalizer

KEY (CORRECT ANSWERS)

1.	B	11.	A
2.	A	12.	A
3.	D	13.	D
4.	C	14.	C
5.	B	15.	C
6.	B	16.	C
7.	C	17.	A
8.	A	18.	C
9.	C	19.	C
10.	D	20.	A

21. C
22. A
23. A
24. B
25. C

EXAMINATION SECTION
TEST 1

DIRECTIONS: Each question or incomplete statement is followed by several suggested answers or completions. Select the one that BEST answers the question or completes the statement. *PRINT THE LETTER OF THE CORRECT ANSWER IN THE SPACE AT THE RIGHT.*

1. Finished art and mechanicals are typically based on the

   A. thumbnail
   B. rough layout
   C. color proof
   D. rough comprehensive

   1.____

2. Which of the following is a DISADVANTAGE associated with the use of offset printing rather than letterpress or gravure?

   A. Usually a slower process overall
   B. More limited in the type of layouts that can be used
   C. Less accommodating of reverses
   D. Less intense inking

   2.____

3. Instructions for a printing job that include the correct page sequence, an identification of all unnumbered pages, layout specifications, and strip-in instructions are gathered collectively on the

   A. master list
   B. assembly sheet
   C. composite
   D. balance sheet

   3.____

4. In Tag Image File Format (TIFF), a pixel is represented by a single bit in

   A. a monochrome picture
   B. binary line art
   C. a binary picture
   D. a grayscale

   4.____

5. In color printing, an undesirable pattern may occur when reproductions are made from halftones, especially if screens are misaligned or at an improper angle. What is the term for this result?

   A. Moiré   B. Hickey   C. Ghosting   D. Slurring

   5.____

6. Which of the following drawing instruments is most appropriate for hand-lettering design?

   A. Hard-lead mechanical pencil
   B. #2 pencil
   C. Razor-point felt-tipped pen
   D. Hardmuth pencil

   6.____

7. Which of the following press types is best for non-paper surfaces?

   A. Gravure
   B. Duplicator offset
   C. Quality offset
   D. Screen

   7.____

8. Which of the following types of finished art is generally preferred because it yields better contrasts for reproduction?

   A. Black-and-white print
   B. Color print
   C. Transparency
   D. Color negative

   8.____

9. If pure, saturated colors are desired as an output, which of the following color correction methods is most appropriate? _____ rendering.

   A. Solid color
   B. Photographic
   C. Presentation graphics
   D. Perceptual

10. The rectangular metal frame in which hot metal type and plates are positioned and locked up for letterpress printing is known as the

    A. platen
    B. chase
    C. quoin
    D. choke

11. Which of the following is used to explain what is presented in a graph, chart, diagram, map, or other technical illustration?

    A. Caption
    B. Legend
    C. Slug line
    D. Cutline

12. What is the printing term for a group of camera-ready layout elements mounted and ready for photographing?

    A. Signature
    B. Composition
    C. Flat
    D. Chain

13. In lithographic platemaking, the process of _____ makes nonimage areas of the plate nonreceptive to ink.

    A. desensitization
    B. etching
    C. stripping
    D. filtering

14. Positioning _____ is typically the first stage in preparing a mechanical dummy for paste-up.

    A. line art
    B. text type
    C. graphics and photography
    D. non-text type

15. Which of the following is a general rule for the design of artwork?

    A. Photographs or illustrations should be positioned so that they face outward from within a page or spread.
    B. Photographs or illustrations with a common horizon should be placed slightly out of alignment.
    C. A *heavy* shot becomes darker as it becomes larger.
    D. Art that is heavy because of bulk or dark tones should be placed low on the page.

16. When a printing press fails to reproduce dots — that is, when no dots are visible — the mechanism is described as

    A. clogged
    B. calendered
    C. plugged
    D. caked

17. When pasting up mechanical artwork for gravure printing, each of the following is a guideline or rule EXCEPT

    A. all elements on the mechanical must be able to tolerate a halftone screen
    B. only one-piece mechanicals can be used for printing
    C. all line work should be included on the basic artwork
    D. transfer shading films should not be used

18. To accomplish quality color printing, accurate positioning of two or more colors of ink is required. This is referred to as

    A. spread   B. register   C. grip   D. lap

19. For each of the following media in an airbrush, it is necessary to use a pressure of 40-50 pounds per square inch (psi) EXCEPT

    A. acrylics   B. dyes   C. lacquers   D. enamels

20. The halftone window of a mechanical is to have a narrow, even margin of white around it to stand out on a screened page. The engraver on the print job will probably prefer that the window be made

    A. by ruling the space in black ink, using no masking film
    B. by using orange or red transparent masking film, taped onto an acetate overlay
    C. with a keyline, drawing the image area on a tissue-paper overlay
    D. by using orange or red transparent masking film, burnished onto the mechanical

21. If one wants to avoid the paste-up stage entirely, which of the following methods should be used to prepare type or graphics for output?

    A. Antialiasing   B. Area composition
    C. Imposition   D. Cropping

22. As a general rule, paper to be die-cut should be of at least a _____-lb. bond or heavier as the design to be die-cut increases in detail.

    A. 10   B. 20   C. 30   D. 40

23. Because of the difficulties associated with its use, _____ should be avoided if possible when adding rules and borders to a mechanical.

    A. a ruling pen   B. transfer art
    C. a typeset line   D. a typeset leader

24. Each of the following is an appropriate use for fine-line markers EXCEPT

    A. accomplishing precise roughs and layouts
    B. rendering small type
    C. marking fold lines
    D. sketching

25. What term is used to describe photographic surfaces which are insensitive to red, but sensitive to ultraviolet, blue, green, yellow, and orange rays?

    A. Polychromatic   B. Panchromatic
    C. Apochromatic   D. Orthochromatic

4 (#1)

KEY (CORRECT ANSWERS)

1. D
2. D
3. B
4. C
5. A

6. D
7. D
8. C
9. C
10. B

11. B
12. C
13. A
14. B
15. D

16. C
17. B
18. B
19. B
20. A

21. B
22. B
23. A
24. C
25. D

———

TEST 2

DIRECTIONS: Each question or incomplete statement is followed by several suggested answers or completions. Select the one that BEST answers the question or completes the statement. *PRINT THE LETTER OF THE CORRECT ANSWER IN THE SPACE AT THE RIGHT.*

1. Which of the following is/are disadvantages associated with the use of clear acetate for overlays?
    I. Does not hold liquid media well
    II. Often becomes discolored with use
    III. May stretch or shrink with temperature
   The CORRECT answer is:

   A. I, II
   B. I, III
   C. II, III
   D. None of the above

2. The main DISADVANTAGE associated with the use of overlays during the preparation of a mechanical is that they

   A. do not mask out areas according to color
   B. may add time later to the process of color separation
   C. may not produce a register that is acceptably close
   D. cannot be used to specify halftones

3. Which of the following characteristics of color is used to describe brightness or dullness?

   A. Saturation
   B. Tone
   C. Hue
   D. Value

4. When working with light sensitive plate coatings, which of the following are most likely to produce a dark reaction? High
    I. humidity
    II. pressure
    III. temperature
   The CORRECT answer is:

   A. I *only*   B. I, II   C. I, III   D. I, II, III

5. What is the term for the type of layout that uses a combination of rectangles (usually illustrations) placed close together?

   A. Mondrian
   B. Omnibus
   C. Copy-heavy
   D. Type-specimen

6. When using a letterpress, what is the protective paper used to cover any part of a printing plate not meant to print?

   A. Crop   B. Frisket   C. Choker   D. Flap

7. In commercial printing applications, halftone screens of between _____ lines/inch are most commonly used.

   A. 50-112   B. 120-166   C. 177-220   D. 245-300

55

8. When burnishing elements in place during the preparation of a mechanical, one should work from

   A. left to right
   B. the center outward
   C. the margins inward
   D. the top down

9. For practical purposes, T-squares used on drawing tables should ideally be

   A. made of wood
   B. made of plastic
   C. made of stainless steel
   D. built into the table

10. In most printing processes using cylinders, the inked plate transfers the image to the paper via the _____ cylinder, which is covered with a rubber sheet.

    A. litho
    B. plate
    C. impression
    D. blanket

11. The most exact way of showing what a final printed product will look like is to compose a(n)

    A. presentation comprehensive
    B. overlay
    C. tight comprehensive
    D. rough layout

12. Which of the following is an inking instrument that is used to compare dimensions or proportions?

    A. Drawing compass
    B. Divider
    C. Ruling pen
    D. Technical pen

13. Which of the following groups of typefaces is also known as Clarendon?

    A. Script
    B. Oldstyle
    C. Sans serif
    D. Slab serif

14. In computer graphics applications, the technique of _____ can be used to simulate gradations of gray by using dot patterns.

    A. aliasing
    B. feathering
    C. dithering
    D. dot etching

15. An artist plans to use Castell 9000 pencils for matt drafting film. Typically, what grades are most appropriate for use in this application?

    A. 8B to IB   B. 8B to 3H   C. 4B to 5H   D. HB to 6H

16. In the print shop, a paper is sometimes run between polished steel rolls to give it desired smoothness. This process is known as

    A. calendering
    B. sizing
    C. caking
    D. slurring

17. To offset the different ink layers in conventional process color separations, halftone screens for yellow should be placed at a _____° angle to one another to avoid undesirable moire patterns.

    A. 45   B. 75   C. 90   D. 105

18. Which of the following would NOT be used as an overprint color? 18.____

    A. Green B. Yellow C. Red D. Blue

19. During color separation, a red filter 19.____

    A. leaves magenta areas of the image transparent
    B. reflects cyan and magenta onto film
    C. leaves cyan areas of the film transparent
    D. reflects yellow and cyan onto film

20. When preparing a mechanical, it is important to remember that the typical gripper margin to be allowed is usually _____ inch, probably at the top or bottom of the sheet. 20.____

    A. 1/4 B. 1/2 C. 1 D. $1\frac{1}{2}$

21. In the rough layout phase of art preparation, the artist should pay close attention to 21.____

    A. trapping
    B. color separation
    C. the weight and size of characters
    D. the photographic art to be used

22. What is the term for a process in which an image is pressed down into the paper surface? 22.____

    A. Engraving   B. Debossing
    C. Embossing   D. Lithography

23. In design, fine-point ball-point pens are most useful for 23.____

    A. mechanical indications for trim, crop, or bleed
    B. trapping
    C. sketching and rendering
    D. drawing dimensions on mechanicals

24. When preparing a mechanical, which of the following may be used to draw guidelines? 24.____
    I. Pencil
    II. Black ink
    III. Nonrepro blue ink
    The CORRECT answer is:

    A. I only   B. I or II
    C. II or III   D. I, II or III

25. Whatever kind of mechanical pencil is chosen for artwork, the lead guard should measure at LEAST _____ long at its shortest point if it is to be used with stencils. 25.____

    A. 0.2 B. 1.75 C. 3.5 D. 5

KEY (CORRECT ANSWERS)

1. B
2. C
3. A
4. C
5. A

6. B
7. B
8. B
9. C
10. D

11. A
12. B
13. D
14. C
15. D

16. A
17. C
18. B
19. C
20. B

21. C
22. B
23. A
24. C
25. C

EXAMINATION SECTION
TEST 1

DIRECTIONS: Each question or incomplete statement is followed by several suggested answers or completions. Select the one that BEST answers the question or completes the statement. *PRINT THE LETTER OF THE CORRECT ANSWER IN THE SPACE AT THE RIGHT.*

1. What is the term for the minimum pressure at which proper ink transfer is possible on a press?

    A. Push-lock
    B. Doctor pressure
    C. Kiss pressure
    D. Pickup point

    1.____

2. Which of the following measuring instruments is equipped with both point and 1/64" increments?

    A. Proportion wheel
    B. Haberule line gauge
    C. Ellipse template
    D. Schaedler precision rule

    2.____

3. Each of the following is an advantage associated with the use of drop-on-demand inkjet printing over continuous inkjet printing EXCEPT

    A. more compact size
    B. higher resolution
    C. quieter operation
    D. lower cost

    3.____

4. Which of the following types of erasers is most appropriate for removing ink and dirt from artwork?

    A. Plastic
    B. Artgum
    C. Pink Pearl
    D. Kneaded rubber

    4.____

5. On high quality projects, which of the following would most likely not be used as an adhesive during paste-up?

    A. Spray adhesive
    B. Rubber cement
    C. Clear tape
    D. Hot wax

    5.____

6. Which of the following is the best material for pasting up negative art?

    A. Kid-finish bristol
    B. Bond paper
    C. Black construction paper
    D. Prepared acetate

    6.____

7. Which of the following materials may be used to form the printing image base on a bimetal printing plate?

    A. Chromium
    B. Copper
    C. Stainless steel
    D. Aluminum

    7.____

8. Which of the following is most appropriate for use with stencils?

    A. Fine line marker
    B. Layout marker
    C. Drafting pen
    D. Rolling writer

    8.____

9. To offset the different ink layers in conventional process color separations, halftone screens for cyan should be placed at a _____ ° angle to one another to avoid undesirable moiré patterns.

   A. 45 B. 75 C. 90 D. 105

10. Which of the following is most appropriate for ruling mechanicals?

    A. Technical pen
    B. Divider
    C. Razor-point felt-tipped pen
    D. Non-repro blue pencil

11. Which of the following brush types include oval-shaped, full brushes that are good for laying broad washes?

    A. Fans B. Sky C. Flats D. Brights

12. Which of the following color conversion methods is most effective for spot colors, and maintains an absolute color match? _____ rendering.

    A. Solid color   B. Photographic
    C. Perceptual   D. Presentation graphics

13. For most applications, the width-to-height ratio for layouts most commonly used is

    A. 1:2 B. 2:3 C. 3:5 D. 1:4

14. Even though dummies are made in numerical or reading sequence, the mechanical of paginated work should probably be done in imposition, so that

    A. allowance is made for *creep* or shingling
    B. facing pages can be visualized together
    C. paste-up is not needlessly slowed
    D. pages will be in order when the signature is ordered and bound

15. In designing artwork and copy for a printed page or board, which of the following ratios of artwork or photography to type is considered the *golden mean*?

    A. 1 to 1 B. 1 to 2 C. 3 to 5 D. 1 to 4

16. Each of the following is an important advantage associated with press proofs EXCEPT

    A. they are made with the actual inks and paper to be used on the job
    B. they can be made quickly and inexpensively
    C. progressive proofs and proof books can be made
    D. multiple proofs can be produced at a reasonable cost

17. Which of the following statements about quality offset printing is FALSE? It

    A. is especially suited to textured paper
    B. is better for flat color reproduction than process color reproduction
    C. offers excellent halftone detail
    D. is generally considered to be the most economic for quality in quantity

18. Digital printing may be used to render an image in which the vertical dimension of the presentation is smaller than the horizontal dimension. This practice is known as

    A. latent-image perspective
    B. landscape orientation
    C. portrait orientation
    D. vanishing-point perspective

19. Which of the following are advantages associated with converting a halftone to a line negative during print making?
    I. Allows full assembly of a piece on the mechanical
    II. Improves image quality
    III. Saves engraver time
    The CORRECT answer is:

    A. I only
    B. I, III
    C. II, III
    D. None of the above

20. Which of the following is a term for the nonprintable area of a print plate?

    A. Layback
    B. Buffer
    C. Gripper margin
    D. Frame

21. The blades used with X-acto knives during mechanical preparation and paste-up are most commonly

    A. #5 and #9
    B. #8 and #10
    C. #11 and #16
    D. #12 and #18

22. Which of the following processes can produce a realistic 2-D image from a 3-D object formation?

    A. Extrusion
    B. Retrenching
    C. Rendering
    D. Extension

23. Which of the following media can be used to produce either line or continuous-tone art?

    A. Marker
    B. Scratchboard
    C. Ink wash
    D. Charcoal

24. In computer graphics, the display space border beyond which graphics display is blanked is known as the

    A. crop margin
    B. ivory board
    C. clip boundary
    D. skip tag

25. What type of mechanical pencil lead is most suitable for use on plastic drafting film?

    A. Graphite
    B. Plastic polymer-based
    C. Simple polymer-based
    D. Oiled graphite

KEY (CORRECT ANSWERS)

1.	C	11.	B
2.	D	12.	A
3.	B	13.	B
4.	A	14.	D
5.	C	15.	C
6.	C	16.	B
7.	B	17.	B
8.	C	18.	B
9.	D	19.	B
10.	A	20.	A

21. C
22. C
23. D
24. C
25. B

TEST 2

DIRECTIONS: Each question or incomplete statement is followed by several suggested answers or completions. Select the one that BEST answers the question or completes the statement. *PRINT THE LETTER OF THE CORRECT ANSWER IN THE SPACE AT THE RIGHT.*

1. Which of the following factors involved in the misregistration of ink in a printed image is most specific to digital applications?

   A. Inaccurate imagesetter generating color separation
   B. Unstable film or stripping material
   C. Platemaking errors
   D. Lack of proper environmental controls

   1.____

2. Typically, _____ typefaces all use diagonal stress.

   A. sans serif   B. script
   C. modern   D. oldstyle

   2.____

3. In computer graphics, the technique of creating a 3-D shape by stretching a 2-D shape along a third axis is known as

   A. solids modeling   B. wireframe modeling
   C. Bézier curving   D. extrusion

   3.____

4. Concerning gouache, which of the following statements is FALSE?

   A. Colors look lighter dry then wet.
   B. It has smoother flow than watercolor.
   C. It is a transparent medium.
   D. High-quality gouache can be used in a pen or airbrush.

   4.____

5. An item of artwork is to be reduced on a mechanical so that its width of 80 picas becomes a finished width of 20 picas. If the reduced image is to be proportional, and the depth of the image is 120 picas, how many picas will the finished depth of the image be?

   A. 15   B. 30   C. 45   D. 60

   5.____

6. The main DISADVANTAGE associated with the use of bitmapped fonts in computer-generated copy is that they

   A. do not scale up and down in size very well
   B. do not permit the use of sans serif fonts
   C. prevent the use of dingbats or symbols
   D. involve the use of complicated algorithms

   6.____

7. A project with _____ color register has two or more opaque colors that don't print closer than 1/16 inch (0.16 cm) of one another.

   A. hairline   B. trapped   C. loose   D. lap

   7.____

8. The purpose of a *slug line* in preparing a mechanical is to indicate

   A. fold lines
   B. the gutter margins
   C. the ruled lines that set type will rest upon
   D. the area that type or artwork is to occupy when set

   8.____

63

9. The process of spacing letters within a line of type is known as

   A. leading   B. kerning   C. serifing   D. plotting

10. During printing, any rollers — whether inking or dampening — which contact a plate are referred to as

    A. blanket cylinders
    C. form rollers
    B. distributing rollers
    D. impression cylinders

11. Which of the following is LEAST likely to create the need for color correction?

    A. Poor lighting conditions at the time the image was photographed
    B. Incorrect exposure when the image was developed
    C. Wrong type of filter used during photography of the image
    D. Incorrect halftone screen angle

12. Photographic surfaces are made sensitive to light by applying salts of either of the following elements EXCEPT

    A. chromium   B. silver   C. copper   D. iron

13. Which of the following types of proofs are directly from the plate negative films before the plates are exposed?

    A. Prepress proofs
    C. Progressive proofs
    B. Press proofs
    D. Blues

14. Which of the following is/are suitable reproduction applications for intaglio printing?
    I. Photographic images
    II. Large, unbroken solids
    III. Fine lines

    The CORRECT answer is:

    A. I only   B. I, II   C. II, III   D. III only

15. What color drawing ink should be used for the trim lines of Mechanicals?

    A. Cobalt blue
    C. Carmine red
    B. Black
    D. Nonrepro blue

16. In CAD/CAM applications, wireframe modeling

    A. automatically removes lines not normally seen from the angle at which the model is viewed
    B. allows the user to determine a drawn object's center of gravity
    C. divides a drawing into color-coded layers that can be selected individually
    D. represents an object as connected points in space

17. A designer wishes to diminish the shadow in a photograph in order to focus attention on the image. Which of the following techniques should be used?

    A. Halftoning
    C. Toning
    B. Vignetting
    D. Spotting

18. Which of the following shading techniques in image processing is a smooth-shading method that computes different colors at the corners of a polygon and then interpolates these colors across the surfaces?
   _____ shading.

   A. Phong   B. Gouraud   C. Smooth   D. Flat

19. The obvious DISADVANTAGE associated with acrylic paints concerns their

   A. covering power
   B. water solubility once dry
   C. versatility on different surfaces
   D. ability to receive overlaid washes

20. The ability of an ink to flow during printing operations is expressed in terms of the ink's

   A. depth   B. length   C. wetness   D. viscosity

21. When expressing the dimensions of art during the preparation of a mechanical, which of the following is a standardized practice?

   A. Expressing dimensions in picas rather than inches or centimeters
   B. Keylining dimensions in an overlay
   C. Listing width first, or underlining it
   D. None of the above

22. What is the term used to describe a color-corrected lens that focuses green, blue, and red in the same plane?

   A. Pantone   B. Astigmatic
   C. Polychromatic   D. Apochromatic

23. Drawing table surfaces for use in commercial art applications should have dimensions of at least

   A. 24" x 30"   B. 30" x 40"   C. 36" x 59"   D. 45" x 90"

24. Which of the following are relief printing processes?
   I. Gravure
   II. Letterpress
   III. Flexography
   IV. Intaglio
   The CORRECT answer is:

   A. I, II   B. II, III
   C. III, IV   D. All of the above

25. Which of the following press types is best for handling tints?

   A. Gravure   B. Duplicator offset
   C. Screen   D. Web

KEY (CORRECT ANSWERS)

1. A
2. D
3. D
4. C
5. B

6. A
7. C
8. D
9. B
10. C

11. D
12. C
13. A
14. D
15. A

16. D
17. B
18. B
19. A
20. B

21. C
22. D
23. B
24. B
25. A

———

EXAMINATION SECTION
TEST 1

DIRECTIONS: Each question or incomplete statement is followed by several suggested answers or completions. Select the one that BEST answers the question or completes the statement. *PRINT THE LETTER OF THE CORRECT ANSWER IN THE SPACE AT THE RIGHT.*

1. You are preparing a press release announcing a cornerstone laying ceremony for a housing project named after a prominent New Yorker. You desire to include in this press release some information about this person's contributions to public housing.
   Of the following sources which are available to you, the BEST one to go to in order to obtain verified information is
   A. the index and issues of a local newspaper obtainable in the public library
   B. Wikipedia
   C. a book on the history of public housing
   D. a biography of the individual

   1.____

2. You have been assigned to prepare a press release announcing the issuance of applications for apartments at a new city housing project.
   Of the following items of information, the one which is LEAST important to include in such a press release is the
   A. average building cost per apartment
   B. rental charges per room
   C. number of apartments in the project
   D. special facilities available at the project

   2.____

3. A company executive has asked you to assist him in preparing a presentation he is to deliver at a city board meeting concerning the potential benefits of a new government computer system. Members of the city administration will be present, as well as the press and the general public.
   Of the following, the theme you should emphasize MOST in this presentation is
   A. faster load times and stronger WiFi in all government buildings
   B. the inadequacies of the current computer system
   C. more efficient processing of city permits, payments and other transactions between the city and residents
   D. benefits of a digitally connected community

   3.____

4. You have been assigned to prepare a nightlife brochure that is to include photos of people dining at area restaurants. However, the photos you have are not adequate, so you run an image search on Google and find more suitable photos to use in the brochure.
   This practice is generally unacceptable because

   4.____

A. readers might notice that the people in the images are not actually dining at area restaurants
B. information on Google is not properly fact-checked
C. photos published on the internet cannot be used in print publications
D. use of the images might violate copyright law

5. It is your job to promote the fact that all pumpkins to be sold at an upcoming Fall Festival are harvested from local farms. Which of the following is the most effective way to ensure residents of the community are aware of this?
    A. Post notes on Twitter and Instagram, and tag the associated farms
    B. Run a print and online "Buy Local" campaign in the weeks leading up to the festival
    C. Publish a series of farmer profiles in the community newspaper
    D. Hang banners over local roads highlighting the festival and its amenities

6. Which of the following, about the opening of a new village dog park, is MOST appropriate according to standard rules of headline writing?
    A. YELPS OF DELIGHT YESTERDAY AS NEW DOG PARK OPENS TO CROWD OF 30 PUPS
    B. NEW FAIRMOUNT DOG PARK OFF TO "RUFF" START
    C. DOGGIE DESTINATION OPENED YESTERDAY IN FAIRMOUNT
    D. MORE BARK THAN BITE: DOG PARK OPENS IN FAIRMOUNT TO HOWLS OF GLORY FROM PUPS AND THEIR OWNERS

7. Suppose that you are assigned to release department information to reporters for the metropolitan press.
    Of the following, the LEAST desirable practice for you to adopt in this assignment is
    A. as a general rule, release information in written form only
    B. set regular dates for the release of department news insofar as possible
    C. secure clearance for the issuance of all written releases
    D. release information first to reporters for newspapers which give the best coverage to department news

8. A letter from a private citizen, complaining about a department policy which has worked a hardship on him, has been referred to you for reply. The citizen asks that this policy be changed.
    In answering this letter, it would be BEST to give major emphasis to
    A. an explanation of the reasons which make such a policy necessary
    B. pointing out that the department regulations cannot be revised to suit each individual case
    C. stating that the operations of any large organization must result in some hardships
    D. inducing the individual to come into the office where the matter can better be dealt with in a face-to-face interview

9. Suppose you are assigned to prepare the annual report for your department. Each bureau has been asked to submit a written report on its activities for the preceding year.
Of the following, the MOST desirable action for you to take in carrying out this assignment is to
   A. return to the bureau heads for revision those reports which, in your opinion, contain unimportant material
   B. rewrite the material submitted by the bureaus to secure improved style without changing content
   C. arrange a conference with the bureau heads to discuss the reports they are to submit
   D. write an introduction and conclusion and let the reports of the bureaus constitute, unaltered, the body of the annual report

10. You have been assigned by your supervisor to do the preliminary editing of material written by other information assistants. After a week in this assignment, you evaluate the material submitted by one information assistant as of lower quality than that of the others.
Of the following, the BEST action for you to take is to
   A. analyze his work with the other information assistants
   B. continue to edit his work without comment at this time
   C. suggest to him that he take a refresher course in writing
   D. recommend his transfer to less original work

11. You have completed gathering the necessary data for a routine newspaper release you are to write.
The MOST desirable step for you to take next is to
   A. write a first draft of the release
   B. work out a plan for the release, including the beginning, the main points, and the ending
   C. develop a suitable title and then begin to write
   D. have someone familiar with the field check the accuracy of the data which you have gathered

12. Of the following writing techniques, the one which is generally LEAST effective for making written material more forceful is the
   A. repetition of a key word or phrase
   B. liberal use of exclamation points, capitalization, underlining and other similar devices
   C. use of the verbs in the active voice, rather than the passive voice
   D. use of a brief sentence, rather than a longer one, to express the same idea

13. The use of anecdotes and other verbal illustrations in writing is desirable PRIMARILY because
   A. this is a good way of showing the author's interest in his subject
   B. the reader will remember the anecdotes
   C. the illustrations will help the reader to remember the author's main idea
   D. the illustrations will entertain the reader

14. You are sending an e-mail to local community groups alerting them to a new youth sports program in municipal parks. It is considered good practice to include links to the department's social media accounts because
    A. it is an opportunity to gain more followers
    B. people respond more favorably to social media links
    C. sports programs are a popular topic on social media
    D. it provides additional outlets for readers to find detailed program information

15. The one of the following which is considered LEAST important in good news-writing is
    A. complete accuracy of names and addresses
    B. full identification of sources of information
    C. strict chronological order of presentation
    D. avoiding the use of editorial statements

16. Of the following, the BEST procedure to follow when writing an article to be read by experts is to
    A. avoid the technical terms as far as possible
    B. explain the technical terms the first time they are used
    C. use the technical terms of the experts
    D. use your literary judgment as to whether to use the technical terms

17. Of the following, the purpose for which it is LEAST important for a writer to have a large vocabulary is to
    A. give him a wider choice of synonyms and antonyms
    B. enable him to express himself in a sophisticated language
    C. improve his reading comprehension
    D. make his writing more exact

18. "The family lived in a small edifice on Maple Street."
    The preceding sentence involves a
    A. good choice of words
    B. poor choice of words because an "edifice" is large rather than small
    C. poor choice of words because the word "edifice" is obsolete
    D. poor choice of words because the word "edifice" is unfamiliar to the average reader

19. In fiction, the BEST way of acquainting the reader with the traits of the characters is through
    A. action
    B. dialogue and description
    C. action and dialogue
    D. dialogue

20. Subheads in an informal pamphlet
    A. are a matter of individual preference
    B. are appropriate only if the subject readily breaks itself down into separate sections
    C. should be used because the pamphlet will be easier to read
    D. should NOT be used because they look "textbookish"

21. The length of an average paragraph should
    A. be about 300 words
    B. harmonize with other elements of a writer's style
    C. not fall below 60 words
    D. vary according to each writing assignment

22. In writing an informational blog post for young readers, it is advisable to include which of the following in order to hold readers' attention?
    A. Bulleted lists
    B. Links to relevant Twitter posts
    C. YouTube and TikTok videos
    D. All of the above

23. Fictitious characters in factual writing should
    A. be disguised to make them appear real
    B. be given names rather than symbols
    C. be given symbols, such as A, B, and C, rather than names
    D. not be used

24. "Clichés should be avoided in writing."
    The one of the following which is NOT a cliché is
    A. "every Tom, Dick and Harry"
    B. "left no stone unturned"
    C. "outrageous possibilities"
    D. "strike while the iron is hot"

25. Public polling indicates that the majority of the American people are unacquainted with such items of general and historical information as the United Nations, the Enron scandal and the Y2K scare.
    Of the following, the MOST probable cause for this lack of knowledge is that
    A. people generally don't read enough to grasp this information
    B. most people don't know anything about current events or international relations
    C. schools avoid the teaching of controversial subjects
    D. this news was not dealt with in the newspapers read by the people polled

26. The *Readers' Guide to Periodical Literature* is
    A. a digit of magazine articles
    B. a literary magazine
    C. an index of magazine articles
    D. an annual guide to magazines

27. To publicize a senior citizens' golf outing hosted by the village parks department, you would likely reach the highest volume of interested participants by running a
    A. Facebook post targeted to seniors living in the state
    B. potentially viral TikTok video
    C. full-page ad in the village newspaper
    D. newspaper profile of the local golf pro

28. All of the following are terms associated with publishing software EXCEPT
    A. point size
    B. click-through rate
    C. stock templates
    D. ePub

29. Your department budget allocated $25,000 this year to be used specifically for digital marketing and promotion. Your supervisor has instructed you to use the money to update and modernize the department's web presence and increase reach. Of the following, the best use of these funds would be to
    A. set up a weekly podcast that features members of the community and how their work relates to the department
    B. improve SEO so that information about the department is more visible when community residents search for it
    C. hire a web designer to lay out a new website
    D. create an ongoing social media campaign that focuses on photos and short videos related to department functions and events in the community

30. The e-mail field used to send a press release to 50 local journalists is
    A. To   B. CC   C. Incognito   D. BCC

31. Of the following sentences, the one which is poorly written because it contains a "dangling construction" is:
    A. After waiting half an hour for the bus, I remembered that I had no money for carfare.
    B. Having returned from our vacations, the supervisor made reassignments.
    C. Smiling pleasantly, she acknowledged the applause of the audience.
    D. Walking over to him, I introduced myself and offered to help him catch his assailant.

Questions 32-36.

DIRECTIONS: Questions 32 through 36 consist of three sentences each. For each question, select the sentence which contains NO error in grammar or usage and write the capital letter preceding that sentence in the space at the right.

32. A. Be sure that everybody brings his notes to the conference.
    B. He looked like he meant to hit the boy.
    C. Mr. Jones is one of the clients who was chosen to represent the district.
    D. All are incorrect.

33. A. He is taller than I.
    B. I'll have nothing to do with these kind of people.
    C. The reason why he will not buy the house is because it is too expensive.
    D. All are incorrect.

34. A. Aren't I eligible for this apartment.
    B. Have you seen him anywheres?
    C. He should of come earlier.
    D. All are incorrect.

35. A. He graduated college in 1982.
    B. He hadn't but one more line to write.
    C. Who do you think is the author of this report?
    D. All are incorrect.

36. A. I talked to one official, whom I knew was fully impartial. 36.____
    B. Everyone signed the petition but him.
    C. He proved not only to be a good student but also a good athlete.
    D. All are incorrect.

Questions 37-40.

DIRECTIONS: Questions 37 through 40 consist of three sentences each. For each item, select the sentence which contains NO error in word usage and write the capital letter preceding that sentence in the space at the right.

37. A. Every year a large amount of tenants are admitted to housing projects. 37.____
    B. Henry Ford owned around a billion dollars in industrial equipment.
    C. He was aggravated by the child's bead behavior.
    D. All are incorrect.

38. A. Before he was committed to the asylum he suffered from the illusion that he was Napoleon. 38.____
    B. Besides stocks, there were also bonds in the safe.
    C. We bet the other team easily.
    D. All are incorrect.

39. A. Bring this report to your supervisor immediately. 39.____
    B. He set the chair down near the table.
    C. The capitol of New York is Albany.
    D. All are incorrect.

40. A. He was chosen to arbitrate the dispute because everyone knew he would be disinterested. 40.____
    B. It is advisable to obtain the best council before making an important decision,
    C. Less college students are interested in teaching than ever before.
    D. All are incorrect.

KEY (CORRECT ANSWERS)

1.	D	11.	B	21.	D	31.	B
2.	A	12.	B	22.	D	32.	A
3.	C	13.	C	23.	B	33.	A
4.	D	14.	D	24.	C	34.	D
5.	B	15.	C	25.	A	35.	C
6.	B	16.	C	26.	C	36.	B
7.	D	17.	B	27.	C	37.	D
8.	A	18.	B	28.	B	38.	B
9.	C	19.	C	29.	D	39.	B
10.	B	20.	C	30.	D	40.	A

TEST 2

DIRECTIONS: Each question or incomplete statement is followed by several suggested answers or completions. Select the one that BEST answers the question or completes the statement. *PRINT THE LETTER OF THE CORRECT ANSWER IN THE SPACE AT THE RIGHT.*

1. "Study your audience and slant your writing toward it." 1.____
   Of the following, the BEST procedure to adopt in applying this principle is to
   A. estimate the intelligence of your audience and write accordingly
   B. use the simplest possible prose style
   C. write about the things you believe your audience wants to read, rather than the things you would prefer to write about
   D. write about what you want to say in the form that is most likely to appeal to your audience

2. "The first rule for giving your writing 'punch' is to take the most important idea and save it until the end of the sentence." 2.____
   Of the following sentences, the one which BEST illustrates this principle is:
   A. After they had notified the police, and had searched the entire neighborhood for hours, they found the little girl in the attic, sleeping peacefully.
   B. The enemy has destroyed the lives of our people, plundered our seas, ravaged our coasts, and burnt our towns.
   C. The thief had stolen the top-secret report, broken open the safe, and rifled the desk.
   D. The tornado left ruin and death in its wake and tore down every building in the village.

3. "America has been built by the cooperative effort of many different kinds of people, working together." 3.____
   In the preceding sentence, a word or phrase which is NOT made superfluous by the use of another word or phrase of similar meaning is
   A. different   B. kinds of
   C. many   D. working together

4. "The company did so well this year that, at the end of the year, it gave each employee a carton of cigarettes, a bottle of wine, and – a $100 bond." 4.____
   In the preceding sentence, the dash
   A. adds more force to the words which follow
   B. detracts from the force of the words which follow
   C. is an illustration of the improper use of punctuation
   D. neither adds nor detracts from the force of the words which follow

5. An e-mail written by another information assistant begins with this sentence: "We beg to acknowledge your note sent to us on the 23rd." It then goes on to reply directly to the matters raised in the note of the 23rd. 5.____

If you are assigned to edit this e-mail for clarity, the MOST desirable action of the following for you to take is to
- A. change the first sentence to read: "We beg to acknowledge your note sent to us on the 23rd and in reply wish to state that...."
- B. leave the first sentence as it is
- C. leave the first sentence unchanged but add another immediately following summarizing what the note of the 23rd inquired about
- D. omit the first sentence in its entirety

6. "Write as you talk" is an axiom widely accepted by news writers. Newspaper readers have a better chance of grasping the news if it is told to them simply and clearly.
The MOST direct implication of the preceding statement is that
- A. an axiom is a statement whose truth is generally accepted by everyone
- B. flowery readers are no different from newspaper reporters
- C. newspaper readers are no different from newspaper reporters
- D. the use of ungrammatical constructions is sometimes justified in writing for the newspapers

6.____

7. "Nowadays, lack of information usually goes hand in hand with little education; similarly, lack of information also usually goes hand in hand with low income. So, if you are writing for people in the lower income brackets or people who haven't gone to college, it's a good guess that they won't have much background knowledge."
The preceding statement implies MOST directly that
- A. little education has always been negatively correlated with little information
- B. poor people are usually not well-informed
- C. people who have not gone to college are in the lower income brackets
- D. writing for the poor and uneducated is more difficult than writing for the rich and well-educated

7.____

8. "Prices of building materials are, in the aggregate, more rigid than those of other commodities. Concentration of control over the supply of goods is frequently advanced as the explanation for price rigidities in general and for building materials in particular."
According to the preceding statement,
- A. increased demand and concurrent fixed supply are frequently responsible for increased prices of building materials
- B. in the aggregate, the high cost of building materials contributes substantially to the high cost of new housing construction
- C. the cost of most articles is generally more flexible than the cost of articles required in the construction of new buildings
- D. the existence of faulty methods of distribution is often advanced as an argument to explain price inequities

8.____

3 (#2)

9. "In undertaking a new development, the builder first decides upon the price or rental range of the dwellings he proposes to construct. Then, after roughly estimating the cost of the selected structure, he tries to find land at suitable prices."
According to the preceding statement,
   A. after a new development is completed, the builder adds up his construction and land costs and fixes the price of the individual house accordingly
   B. it is difficult to predict the probable cost of a new dwelling unit because of constant fluctuation in the cost of building materials
   C. land costs influence the selling price of dwellings least
   D. the selling price of a house is usually determined before construction is begun

9.____

10. "A construction program initiated by public agencies better protects the home buyer and insures the greater soundness of the neighborhood."
According to the preceding statement,
   A. a home buyer is more confident of the safety of his investment if he is given to understand that the neighborhood will not change
   B. a public agency is more responsible in construction programs than a private builder could hope to be
   C. since a public agency can, if necessary, control the development of a neighborhood through zoning laws, public housing is more desirable
   D. to ensure the soundness of a neighborhood it is more effective to have the building of new homes planned by public agencies

10.____

11. "To achieve sound planning we cannot rely on educating the builder to the fact that what is good for the public will be ultimately good for him, for his interest is usually short term and the pattern in which he functions is not set up for voluntary reform."
According to the preceding statement,
   A. a builder is not interested in educating the public to its ultimate benefits
   B. builders whose interests are usually of short duration can be educated to set up voluntary reforms
   C. since a builder's interest in any property is usually of short duration, he will voluntarily function for public benefit
   D. we cannot rely on educating a builder to the fact that public benefit is to his advantage in the long run

11.____

12. "If cities had a long-range objective, if they had plans showing the expected line of growth, plans for their future schools and parks, their houses and their locations, their industries and their locations, their future transportation facilities and their utilities, then with the advent of an emergency requiring government spending they could channel the expenditures and step up the program along the lines of the larger long-term plans."

12.____

According to the preceding statement,
- A. a city wishing to eliminate slums can with proper planning take advantage of an emergency requiring the channeling of expenditures
- B. an emergency requires the channeling of expenditures so that greater efficiency can be shown in planning
- C. cities which have long-range plans can make better use of the funds spent by the government during a depression
- D. long-range objectives help a city to devise new plans for the development of parks, schools, and other public improvements at a considerable saving

13. "Increment or decrement in city income hangs largely upon the maintenance of the values and valuations of real property, upon the quantity of new improvements that go into the city, upon the profitableness of real estate, upon the advent of booms and depressions, and upon the flow of people into or out of the city."
According to the preceding statement,
- A. a boom or a depression has a marked effect on the flow of people into or out of a city
- B. new improvements that go into a city enhance the profitableness of real estate
- C. real estate values, which form the major basis of a city's taxation, are the sources of city salaries
- D. the valuation of a city's income depends on the values of the real estate in the city

14. "The institution of the family is a vitally important part of all human societies, but in modern society, particularly, various organized services have developed that enable some people to secure some of the most essential benefits of family life without belonging to a family group."
Of the following, the LEAST valid inference on the basis of the preceding statement is that
- A. people who are not part of a family unit can obtain most of the essential benefits of family life by contacting an appropriate social agency
- B. present day society offers an opportunity to some who are not members of a family unit to share in some of the benefits of family living
- C. the institution of the family is not native to modern society alone
- D. to obtain the benefits of family life it is usually necessary to belong to a family group

15. "Reform organizations seek, as a rule, to bring about a specific economic or political change; social work agencies are usually occupied with the task of meeting existing situations in the lives of particular individuals or groups."
According to the preceding statement,
- A. a reform organization is concerned with helping the individual by changing some factor in the environment which the individual feels is too arduous to accept
- B. a reform organization is not concerned with the ability of the individual to meet his social responsibilities

C. social work agencies are not concerned with any specific economic or political change because this does not involve the individual's personal adjustment
D. social workers are primarily concerned with helping their clients to meet current living conditions

16. "Adequate facilities for education, recreation and health must be provided for children, and social conditions created that promote the child's development into law-abiding citizens. It is not the task of social work to provide these facilities but to direct children to them and to help them to use these facilities."
Of the following, the MOST accurate statement on the basis of the preceding statement is that
    A. A child who does not have adequate educational, recreational and health facilities will develop into a poor citizen
    B. the education of the public to the importance of providing adequate facilities for children is primarily the social worker's responsibility
    C. the proper use of leisure time by children is an important aspect of the social worker's job
    D. the three most important needs of a child which must be satisfied first are those of education, recreation and health

16.____

17. "Social workers start from the assumption that preservation of the family as the basic unit of social living is their accepted objective. In view of the frequency of divorce and the breakdown of authority in the home, social work now makes articulate its concern for family integrity."
According to the preceding statement,
    A. failure to keep the family as a basic unit leads to a breakdown of authority in the home, upsetting family integrity
    B. in extreme cases where divorce is inevitable a social worker must accept the breakdown of the family unit
    C. social workers are primarily concerned with keeping a family together as a basis entity of social living
    D. the importance of the family to society has been demonstrated by experience with children who have been institutionalized

17.____

18. "The marked change in the spirit in which social work is carried on is evidenced in the adoption of business methods of organization, including centralized purchasing of supplies for social agencies, cost accounting, careful budgeting and auditing of accounts, evaluation of methods and publication of reports. Trained personnel for defined jobs is increasingly sought, and there is appreciation of the differentiated abilities required in the social agency."
According to the preceding statement,
    A. it is apparent that the adoption of business methods of organization has resulted in a change in the method of preparing case work reports
    B. social work agencies that train people for definite jobs achieve savings in social work that approximate those of business organization

18.____

C. social work now uses current business procedures in carrying forward the purposes of a social agency
D. trained personnel in social work are responsible for the adoption of business methods of procedure

19. "Basic to the functioning of the professional social worker is an understanding of human personality and of the world we live in."
The one of the following which is the MOST accurate statement on the basis of the preceding quotation is that
   A. a social worker must be familiar with human behavior in order to be able to perform his work properly
   B. a social worker who understands human personality is able to function better as a citizen of the world
   C. social work may be classified as a profession because, for its proper performance, a basic understanding of the social and biological sciences is required
   D. through his daily contact with his clients a social worker will obtain a better understanding of the world he lives in

19._____

Questions 20-24.

DIRECTIONS: Questions 20 through 24 each consist of three words. For each item, select the word which is INCORRECTLY spelled and write the capital letter preceding that word in the space at the right.

20. A. achievment   B. maintenance   20._____
    C. questionnaire   D. all are correct

21. A. prevelant   B. pronunciation   21._____
    C. separate   D. all are correct

22. A. permissible   B. relevant   22._____
    C. seize   D. all are correct

23. A. corroborate   B. desparate   23._____
    C. eighth   D. all are correct

24. A. exceed   B. feasibility   24._____
    C. psycological   D. all are correct

7 (#2)

Questions 25-29.

DIRECTIONS: Questions 25 through 29 are to be answered on the basis of the following information.

Copy I is an accurate copy of material which is to be prepared for the printer. Copy II of this material contains a number of typographical errors. Compare Copy II with Copy I and find the typographical errors. Every group of four lines in Copy II is numbered. Indicate the number of typographical errors in each group of lines of Copy II by writing in the correspondingly numbered space at the right the capital letter preceding the best of the following alternatives.

- A. No errors
- B. 1-2 errors
- C. 3-4 errors
- D. 5 or more errors

COPY I

Parcel 1. Beginning at a point formed by the intersection of the northerly side of 73rd avenue with the westerly side of Francis Lewis boulevard as said streets are indicated upon the final map of the borough of Queens known as Alteration Map No. 2831 adopted by the board of estimate on May 15, 1941; running thence northerly along the westerly side of Francis Lewis boulevard following a curve having a radius of 8,053 feet for a distance of 585.15 feet; thence northerly along the westerly side of Francis Lewis boulevard in a straight line for a distance of 687.43 feet; thence northerly along the westerly side of Francis Lewis boulevard and its prolongation following a curve having a radius of 5.667 feet for a distance of 509.79 feet to the old southerly side of North Hempstead turnpike as formerly laid out and as shown discontinued upon the aforementioned final city map; thence easterly along said southerly side of North Hempstead turnpike for 110.12 feet to the easterly side of Francis Lewis boulevard; thence southerly along the easterly side of Francis Lewis boulevard following a curve having a radius of 5.783 feet for a distance of 489.20 feet; thence southerly along the easterly side of Francis Lewis boulevard in a straight line for a distance of 687.43 feet; thence southerly along the easterly side of Francis Lewis boulevard following a curve having a radius of 7,947 feet for a distance of 572.90 feet to the northerly side of 73rd avenue.

COPY II

25. Parcel 1. Beginning at point formed by the intersection of the northerly side of 73rd Avenue with the westerly side of Francis Lewis boulevard as said streets are indicated upon the final map of the borough of Queens known as Alteration Map No. 2831 adapted by the board of estimate on May15, 1941;   25.____

26. running thence northerly along the westerly side of Francis Lewis boulevard following a curve having a radius of 8,053 feet for a distance of 585.15 feet; thence northerly along the westerly side of Francis Lewis boulevard in a straight line for a distance of 687.43 feet; thence northerly along   26.____

27. the westerly side of Francis Lewis boulevard and its prolongation following a curve having a radius of 5.677 feet for a distance of 509.79 feet to the old southerly side of North Hempstead Turnpike as formerly laid out and is shown discontinued upon the aforementioned final city map; thence easterly   27.____

28. along said southerly side of North Hempstead turnpike for 1101.2 feet to the easterly side of Francis Lewis boulevard; thence southerly along the easterly side of Francis Lewis boulevard following a curve having a radius of 5.783 feet for a distance of 489.20 feet; thence southerly along the easterly

29. side of Francis Lewis boulevard in a straight line for a distance of 687.43 feet; thence southerly along the easterly side of Francis Lewis boulevard following a curve having a radius of 7,947 feet for a distance of 572.09 feet to the northerly side of 73rd avenue.

30. "He described a hypothetical situation to illustrate his point."
In the preceding sentence, the word "hypothetical" means MOST NEARLY
   A. actual   B. theoretical   C. typical   D. unusual

31. "I gave tacit approval to my partner's proposed business changes."
In the preceding sentence, the word "tacit" means MOST NEARLY
   A. enthusiastic   B. partial   C. silent   D. written

32. "Jones was considered an astute lawyer by the members of his profession."
In the preceding sentence, the word "astute" means MOST NEARLY
   A. clever   B. persevering
   C. poorly trained   D. unethical

33. "There were intimations even in early days of the way in which he would go."
In the preceding sentence, the word "intimations" means MOST NEARLY
   A. hints   B. patterns   C. plans   D. purposes

34. "His last book was published posthumously."
In the preceding sentence, the word "posthumously" means MOST NEARLY
   A. after the death of the author   B. printed free by the publisher
   C. without a dedication   D. without royalties

35. "When he was challenged, he used every known subterfuge."
In the preceding sentence, the word "subterfuge" means MOST NEARLY
   A. evasion to justify one's conduct
   B. means of attack to defend one's self
   C. medical device
   D. unconscious thought

36. "His partner suggested a course of action that would alleviate the difficulties which confronted him."
In the preceding sentence, the word "alleviate" means MOST NEARLY
   A. correct   B. lessen   C. remove   D. solve

37. "Among the applicants for the new apartment white-collar workers were preponderant."
In the preceding sentence, the word "preponderant" means MOST NEARLY
   A. considered not eligible   B. in evidence
   C. superior in number   D. the first to apply

38. "The captain gave a lucid explanation of his plans for the coming campaign." 38.____
In the preceding sentence, the word "lucid" means MOST NEARLY
   A. clear   B. graphic   C. interesting   D. thorough

39. "He led a sedentary life." 39.____
In the preceding sentence, the word "sedentary" means MOST NEARLY
   A. aimless   B. exciting   C. full   D. inactive

40. "His plan for the next campaign was very plausible." 40.____
In the preceding sentence, the word "plausible" means MOST NEARLY
   A. appropriate   B. believable   C. usable   D. valuable

KEY (CORRECT ANSWERS)

1.	D	11.	D	21.	A	31.	C
2.	A	12.	C	22.	D	32.	A
3.	C	13.	D	23.	B	33.	A
4.	A	14.	A	24.	C	34.	A
5.	D	15.	D	25.	C	35.	A
6.	B	16.	C	26.	A	36.	B
7.	B	17.	C	27.	C	37.	C
8.	C	18.	C	28.	B	38.	A
9.	D	19.	A	29.	B	39.	D
10.	D	20.	A	30.	B	40.	B

PREPARING WRITTEN MATERIAL

PARAGRAPH REARRANGEMENT
COMMENTARY

The sentences that follow are in scrambled order. You are to rearrange them in proper order and indicate the letter choice containing the correct answer at the space at the right.

Each group of sentences in this section is actually a paragraph presented in scrambled order. Each sentence in the group has a place in that paragraph; no sentence is to be left out. You are to read each group of sentences and decide upon the best order in which to put the sentences so as to form a well-organized paragraph.

The questions in this section measure the ability to solve a problem when all the facts relevant to its solution are not given.

More specifically, certain positions of responsibility and authority require the employee to discover connection between events sometimes, apparently, unrelated. In order to do this, the employee will find it necessary to correctly infer that unspecified events have probably occurred or are likely to occur. This ability becomes especially important when action must be taken on incomplete information.

Accordingly, these questions require competitors to choose among several suggested alternatives, each of which presents a different sequential arrangement of the events. Competitors must choose the MOST logical of the suggested sequences.

In order to do so, they may be required to draw on general knowledge to infer missing concepts or events that are essential to sequencing the given events. Competitors should be careful to infer only what is essential to the sequence. The plausibility of the wrong alternatives will always require the inclusion of unlikely events or of additional chains of events which are NOT essential to sequencing the given events.

It's very important to remember that you are looking for the best of the four possible choices, and that the best choice of all may not even be one of the answers you're given to choose from.

There is no one right way to solve these problems. Many people have found it helpful to first write out the order of the sentences, as they would have arranged them, on their scrap paper before looking at the possible answers. If their optimum answer is there, this can save them some time. If it isn't, this method can still give insight into solving the problem. Others find it most helpful to just go through each of the possible choices, contrasting each as they go along. You should use whatever method feels comfortable and works for you.

While most of these types of questions are not that difficult, we've added a higher percentage of the difficult type, just to give you more practice. Usually there are only one or two questions on this section that contain such subtle distinctions that you're unable to answer confidently. And you then may find yourself stuck deciding between two possible choices, neither of which you're sure about.

EXAMINATION SECTION
TEST 1

DIRECTIONS: Each group of sentences in this section is actually a paragraph presented in scrambled order. Each sentence in the group has a place in that paragraph; no sentence is to be left out. You are to read each group of sentences so as to form a well-organized paragraph. Before trying to answer the questions which follow each group of sentences, jot down the correct order of the sentences. Then answer each of the questions by printing the letter of the correct answer in the space at the right. Remember that you will receive credit only for answers marked.

P. It is unfounded because, while the weak resent the power of the strong, they also respect it.
Q. The hesitancy stems from a concern for public opinion in other countries.
R. The United States has ordinarily been ill at ease in using its military power in support of its interests.
S. The concern is largely unfounded.
T. The roots of American hesitancy are deeply imbedded in the American mind.

1. Which sentence did you put last?
   A. P   B. Q   C. R   D. S   E. T

2. Which sentence did you put after Sentence R?
   A. P
   B. Q
   C. S
   D. T
   E. None of the above. Sentence R is last.

3. Which sentence did you put before Sentence S?
   A. P
   B. Q
   C. R
   D. T
   E. None of the above. Sentence S is first.

4. Which sentence did you put before Sentence R?
   A. P
   B. Q
   C. S
   D. T
   E. None of the above. Sentence R is first.

5. Which sentence did you put fourth?
    A. P B. Q C. R D. S E. T

KEY (CORRECT ANSWERS)

1. A
2. D
3. B
4. E
5. D

TEST 2

DIRECTIONS: Each group of sentences in this section is actually a paragraph presented in scrambled order. Each sentence in the group has a place in that paragraph; no sentence is to be left out. You are to read each group of sentences so as to form a well-organized paragraph. Before trying to answer the questions which follow each group of sentences, jot down the correct order of the sentences. Then answer each of the questions by printing the letter of the correct answer in the space at the right. Remember that you will receive credit only for answers marked.

P. Its lawlessness was virtually non-existent.
Q. The *Old West*, as portrayed in motion pictures, on television, and in books, is completely distorted.
R. It is obvious, therefore, that the *Old West* is falsely presented in mass media solely for commercial purposes.
S. Its heroes, too, were far from heroic.
T. Those who lived in the *Old West* in its final days, or talked to oldtimers, know the truth.

1. Which sentence did you put last?
   A. P   B. Q   C. R   D. S   E. T

2. Which sentence did you put after Sentence Q?
   A. P
   B. R
   C. S
   D. T
   E. None of the above. Sentence Q is last.

3. Which sentence did you put before Sentence S?
   A. P
   B. Q
   C. R
   D. T
   E. None of the above. Sentence S is first.

4. Which sentence did you put before Sentence Q?
   A. P
   B. R
   C. S
   D. T
   E. None of the above. Sentence Q is first.

2 (#2)

5. Which sentence did you put after Sentence S?   5.____
   A. P
   B. Q
   C. R
   D. T
   E. None of the above. Sentence S is last.

KEY (CORRECT ANSWERS)

1. C
2. D
3. A
4. E
5. C

TEST 3

DIRECTIONS: Each group of sentences in this section is actually a paragraph presented in scrambled order. Each sentence in the group has a place in that paragraph; no sentence is to be left out. You are to read each group of sentences so as to form a well-organized paragraph. Before trying to answer the questions which follow each group of sentences, jot down the correct order of the sentences. Then answer each of the questions by printing the letter of the correct answer in the space at the right. Remember that you will receive credit only for answers marked.

P. One advertising executive became agitated recently when he suddenly realized that the floors of supermarkets were being unimaginatively used merely to walk on.
Q. Blank spaces, advertising men feel, cry out to be filled with merchandise-hustling messages.
R. He invented a slide projector which projects images on sheets of translucent plastic embedded in supermarket floors.
S. At once, he got to work to correct this unforgiveable oversight.
T. As nature abhors a vacuum, so do advertising men decry blank spaces.

1. Which sentence did you put last?
   A. P
   B. Q
   C. S
   D. T
   E. None of the above. Sentence R is last.

2. Which sentence did you put third?
   A. P   B. Q   C. R   D. S   E. T

3. Which sentence did you put before Sentence T?
   A. P
   B. Q
   C. R
   D. T
   E. None of the above. Sentence T is first.

4. Which sentence did you put after Sentence P?
   A. Q
   B. R
   C. S
   D. T
   E. None of the above. Sentence P is last.

5. Which sentence did you put before Sentence Q?　　　　　　　　　　　　5.____
   A. P
   B. R
   C. S
   D. T
   E. None of the above. Sentence Q is last.

KEY (CORRECT ANSWERS)

1. E
2. A
3. E
4. C
5. D

TEST 4

DIRECTIONS: Each group of sentences in this section is actually a paragraph presented in scrambled order. Each sentence in the group has a place in that paragraph; no sentence is to be left out. You are to read each group of sentences so as to form a well-organized paragraph. Before trying to answer the questions which follow each group of sentences, jot down the correct order of the sentences. Then answer each of the questions by printing the letter of the correct answer in the space at the right. Remember that you will receive credit only for answers marked.

P. It is estimated that Americans smoked almost a trillion cigarettes in 2020, while they smoked only several hundred million cigars and pipefuls of tobacco.
Q. Originally, they were considered exclusively a *ladies'* smoke.
R. Only in this century did cigarettes become popular in the United States.
S. Far more Americans smoke cigarettes today than smoke cigars and pipes combined.
T. This was not always the case, however.

1. Which sentence did you put first?   1.____
   A. P   B. Q   C. R   D. S   E. T

2. Which sentence did you put after Sentence Q?   2.____
   A. P
   B. R
   C. S
   D. T
   E. None of the above. Sentence Q is last.

3. Which sentence did you put before Sentence T?   3.____
   A. P
   B. Q
   C. R
   D. S
   E. None of the above. Sentence T is last.

4. Which sentence did you put after Sentence R?   4.____
   A. P
   B. Q
   C. S
   D. T
   E. None of the above. Sentence R is last.

5. Which sentence did you put before Sentence R? 5.____
   A. P
   B. Q
   C. S
   D. T
   E. None of the above. Sentence R is first.

KEY (CORRECT ANSWERS)

1. D
2. E
3. A
4. B
5. D

TEST 5

DIRECTIONS: Each group of sentences in this section is actually a paragraph presented in scrambled order. Each sentence in the group has a place in that paragraph; no sentence is to be left out. You are to read each group of sentences so as to form a well-organized paragraph. Before trying to answer the questions which follow each group of sentences, jot down the correct order of the sentences. Then answer each of the questions by printing the letter of the correct answer in the space at the right. Remember that you will receive credit only for answers marked.

P. A *megagram*, or a million *grams*, is, therefore, equal to 2.205 pounds.
Q. A *gram* is equivalent to 1/28.35 ounces.
R. The fundamental unit of mass in the metric system is the *gram*.
S. A *kilogram*, or a thousand *grams*, is equal to 2.205 pounds.
T. *Gram* is derived from the late Greek, *gramma*, meaning a *small weight*.

1. Which sentence did you put after Sentence S?
   A. P
   B. Q
   C. R
   D. T
   E. None of the above. Sentence S is last.

2. Which sentence did you put before Sentence T?
   A. P
   B. Q
   C. R
   D. S
   E. None of the above. Sentence T is first.

3. Which sentence did you put after Sentence Q?
   A. P
   B. R
   C. S
   D. T
   E. None of the above. Sentence Q is last.

4. Which sentence did you put before Sentence R?
   A. P
   B. Q
   C. S
   D. T
   E. None of the above. Sentence R is first.

5. Which sentence did you put after Sentence T? 5.____
   A. P
   B. Q
   C. R
   D. S
   E. None of the above. Sentence T is last.

KEY (CORRECT ANSWERS)

1. A
2. C
3. C
4. E
5. B

PREPARING WRITTEN MATERIAL
EXAMINATION SECTION
TEST 1

DIRECTIONS: Each of the following sentences may be classified under one of the following four categories:
A. *Faulty* because of incorrect grammar or usage
B. *Faulty* because of incorrect punctuation or spelling
C. *Faulty* because of incorrect capitalization
D. *Correct*

Examine each sentence carefully. Then, in the correspondingly numbered space on the right, print the capital letter preceding the option which is the best of the four suggested above.

(All incorrect sentences contain but one type of error. Consider a sentence correct if it contains none of the types of errors mentioned, even though there may be other correct ways of expressing the same thought.

1. They gave the poor man some food when he approached. 1._____
2. I regret the loss caused by the error. 2._____
3. The students have a new teacher for shop mantenance. 3._____
4. They sweared to bring out all the facts. 4._____
5. He decided to open a branch store on 33rd street. 5._____
6. His speed is equal and more than that of a racehorse. 6._____
7. He felt very warm on that Summer day. 7._____
8. He was assisted by his friend, who lives in the next house. 8._____
9. The climate of New York is colder than California. 9._____
10. I shall wait for you on the corner. 10._____
11. Did we see the boy whose the leader? 11._____
12. Being a modest person, John seldom takes about his invention. 12._____
13. The gang is called the smith street boys. 13._____
14. He seen the man break into the store. 14._____

2 (#1)

15. We expected to lay still there for quite a while. 15.____
16. He is considered to be the Leader of his organization. 16.____
17. Although He received an invitation, He won't go. 17.____
18. The letter must be here some place. 18.____
19. I thought it to be he. 19.____
20. We expect to remain here for a long time. 20.____
21. The committee was agreed. 21.____
22. Two-thirds of the building are finished. 22.____
23. The water was froze. 23.____
24. Everyone of the salesmen must supply their own car. 24.____
25. Who is the author of Gone With the Wind? 25.____
26. He marched on and declaring that he would never surrender. 26.____
27. Who shall I say called? 27.____
28. Everyone has left but they. 28.____
29. Who did we give the order to? 29.____
30. Send your order in immediately. 30.____
31. I believe I paid the Bill. 31.____
32. I have not met but one person. 32.____
33. Why aren't Tom, and Fred, going to the dance? 33.____
34. What reason is there for him not going? 34.____
35. The seige of Malta was a tremendous event. 35.____
36. I was there yesterday I assure you. 36.____
37. Your ukulele is better than mine. 37.____
38. No one was there only Mary. 38.____

3 (#1)

39. The Capital city of Vermont is Montpelier. 39.____

40. Reggie Jackson may hit the largest amount of home runs this season. 40.____

KEY (CORRECT ANSWERS)

1.	B	11.	B	21.	D	31.	C
2.	D	12.	D	22.	A	32.	A
3.	B	13.	C	23.	A	33.	B
4.	A	14.	A	24.	A	34.	A
5.	C	15.	A	25.	B	35.	B
6.	A	16.	C	26.	A	36.	B
7.	C	17.	C	27.	D	37.	B
8.	D	18.	A	28.	D	38.	A
9.	A	19.	A	29.	A	39.	C
10.	D	20.	D	30.	D	40.	A

TEST 2

Questions 1-3.

DIRECTIONS: Questions 1 through 3 each consist of four sentences. Choose the one sentence in each set of four that would be BEST for a formal letter or report. Consider grammar and appropriate usage.

1. A. Most all the work he completed before he become ill.
   B. He completed most of the work before becoming ill.
   C. Prior to him becoming ill his work was mostly completed.
   D. Before he became will most of the work he had completed.

   1.____

2. A. Being that the report lacked a clearly worded recommendation, it did not matter that it contained enough information.
   B. There was enough information in the report, although it, including the recommendation, were not clearly worded.
   C. Although the report contained enough information, it did not have a clearly worded recommendation.
   D. Though the report did not have a recommendation that was clearly worded, and the information therein contained was enough.

   2.____

3. A. Having already overlooked the important mistakes, the ones which she found were not as important toward the end of the letter.
   B. Toward the end of the letter she had already overlooked the important mistakes, so that which she had found were not important.
   C. The mistakes which she had already overlooked were not as important as those which near the end of letter she had found.
   D. The mistakes which she found near the end of the letter were not so important as those which she had already overlooked.

   3.____

Questions 4-5.

DIRECTIONS: Select the correct answer.

4. The unit has exceeded _____ goals and the employees are satisfied with _____ accomplishments.
   A. their; it's   B. it's, it's   C. is, there   D. its, their

   4.____

5. Research indicates that employees who _____ no opportunity for close social relationships often find their work unsatisfying, and this _____ of satisfaction often reflects itself in low production.
   A. have, lack   B. have, excess   C. has, lack   D. has, excess

   5.____

KEY (CORRECT ANSWERS)

1. B
2. C
3. D
4. D
5. A

TEST 3

DIRECTIONS: Select the choice which BEST expresses the thought and which contains NO errors in grammar or sentence construction.

1.
   A. She, hearing a signal, the source lamp flashed.
   B. While hearing a signal, the source lamp flashed
   C. In hearing a signal, the source lamp flashed.
   D. As she heard a signal, the source lamp flashed.

2.
   A. Every one of the time records have been initialed in the designated spaces.
   B. All of the time records has been initialed in the designated spaces.
   C. Which one of the time records was initialed in the designated spaces.
   D. The time records all been initialed in the designated spaces.

3.
   A. If there is no one else to answer the phone, you will have to answer it.
   B. You will have to answer it yourself if no one else answers the phone.
   C. If no one else is not around to pick up the phone, you have to do it.
   D. You will have to answer the phone when nobodys here to do it.

4.
   A. Dr. Byrnes not in his office. What could I do for you?
   B. Dr. Byrnes is not in his office. Is there something I can do for you?
   C. Since Dr. Byrnes is not in his office, might there be something I may do for you?
   D. Is there any ways I can assist you since Dr. Brynes is not in his office?

5.
   A. She do not understand how the new console works.
   B. The way the new console works, she doesn't understand.
   C. She doesn't understand how the new console works.
   D. The new console works, so that she doesn't understand.

KEY (CORRECT ANSWERS)

1. D
2. C
3. A
4. B
5. C

TEST 4

DIRECTIONS: The following questions each consist of a sentence which may or may not be an example of good English usage.

Consider grammar, punctuation, spelling, capitalization, awkwardness, etc.

Examine each sentence and then choose the correct statement about it from the four choices below. If the English usage in the sentence given is better than any of the changes suggested in options B, C, or D, choose option A. (Do not choose an option that will change the meaning of the sentence.)

1. The typist used an extention cord in order to connect her typewriter to the outlet nearest to her desk.
   A. This is an example of acceptable writing.
   B. A period should be placed after the word "cord" and the word "in" should have a capital "I."
   C. A comma should be placed after the word "typewriter."
   D. The word "extention" should be spelled "extension."

2. He would have went to the conference if he had received an invitation.
   A. This is an example of acceptable writing.
   B. The word "went" should be replaced by the word "gone."
   C. The word "had" should be replaced by "would have."
   D. The word "conference" should be spelled "conference."

3. In order to make the report neater, he spent many hours rewriting it.
   A. This is an example of acceptable writing.
   B. The word "more" should be inserted before the word "neater."
   C. There should be a colon after the word "neater."
   D. The word "spent" should be changed to "have spent."

4. His supervisor told him that he should of read the memorandum more carefully.
   A. This is an example of acceptable writing.
   B. The word "memorandum" should be spelled "memorandom."
   C. The word "of" should be replaced by the word "have."
   D. The word "carefully" should be replaced by the word "have."

5. It was decided that two separate reports should be written.
   A. This is an example of acceptable writing.
   B. A comma should be inserted after the word "decided."
   C. The word "be" should be replaced by the word "been."
   D. A colon should be inserted after the word "that."

6. She don't seem to understand that the work must be done as soon as possible.
   A. This is an example of acceptable writing.
   B. The word "doesn't" should replace the word "don't."
   C. The word "why" should replace the word "that."
   D. The word "as" before the word "soon" should be eliminated.

KEY (CORRECT ANSWERS)

1. D
2. B
3. A
4. C
5. A
6. B

ENGLISH EXPRESSION
CHANGE IN CONSTRUCTION

COMMENTARY

A searching type of multiple-choice question requires the candidate to revise a sentence according to the directions provided for that sentence and choose the word or phrase that will appear in the best revision.

Fundamentally, this question attempts to measure the candidate's ability to re-write or to manipulate a sentence or statement with grammatical correctness, felicity of expression, flexibility in construction, and facility of substitution.

This is actually a subtle method of employing the multiple-choice question to achieve the evaluations ordinarily directly obtained through the traditional essay-writing question.

SAMPLE QUESTIONS

DIRECTIONS: In questions 1 and 2, you are given a complete sentence which you are to rewrite in your mind, starting with the words given just below it.

Make whatever changes the new sentence plan requires, but no others; do not change the overall meaning of the sentence.

Note that you are not correcting a mistake in the original sentence; you are simply changing the construction. The revised sentence should be grammatically correct, but it need not necessarily be a better way of expressing the meaning.

There may be more than one way of recasting the sentence but only one will enable you to answer the question.

Read the directions for each question carefully. They may specify that the missing word or expression appear somewhere in the rewritten sentence; they may ask for the next word in the rewritten sentence, the word following a specific word, etc.

1. Most people acquire about 75 percent of what they learn through the sense of sight.
   REWRITTEN: About 75 percent ....
   Somewhere in the part of the rewritten sentence indicated by dots is the word

   A. them B. acquired C. a D. learning E. study

   ACCEPTABLY REWRITTEN, the above sentence would read:
   About 75 percent of what most people learn is acquired through the sense of sight.
   You would, therefore, mark B on your answer sheet.

2. Various studies show that a great amount of the absenteeism in factories is caused by preventable accidents.
   REWRITTEN: According to various studies, preventable accidents ...
   The NEXT WORDS in the rewritten sentence are

   A. result from B. could be C. are caused by
   D. are related to E. account for

   ACCEPTABLY REWRITTEN, the above sentence would read:
   According to various studies, preventable accidents account for the great amount of absenteeism in factories.
   You would, therefore, mark E on your answer sheet.

EXAMINATION SECTION
TEST 1

DIRECTIONS: In the following questions, you are given a complete sentence which you are to rewrite in your mind, starting with the words given just below it. Make whatever changes the new sentence plan requires, but no others; do not change the overall meaning of the sentence.

Note that you are not correcting a mistake in the original sentence; you are simply changing the construction. The revised sentence should be grammatically correct, but it need not necessarily be a better way of expressing the meaning. There may be more than one way of recasting the sentence but only one will enable you to answer the question.

Read the directions for each question carefully. They may specify that the missing word or expression appear somewhere in the rewritten sentence; they may ask for the next word in the rewritten sentence, the word following a specific word, etc.

1. As a literary genre, the messianic drama falls into the category of myth or romance, for its central figure conforms to the definitions supplied by Northrup Frye, in THE ANATOMY OF CRITICISM, of the mythic hero.
   REWRITTEN:
      Because its central figure conforms to the definitions of the mythic hero supplied by Northrup Frye, in THE ANATOMY OF CRITICISM, the messianic drama is ....
   The *NEXT* word in the rewritten sentence is

   A. into   B. literary   C. categorized
   D. categorically E. a

2. In THE EMPEROR JULIAN, the second part of the drama, Ibsen reveals Julian to be a false Messiah.
   REWRITTEN:
      Julian is .....
   Somewhere in the part of the rewritten sentence indicated by dots is the word

   A. reveals   B. by   C. falsified
   D. in which   E. messianic

3. More interesting, because more subtly hidden, is Chekhov's use of melodrama.
   REWRITTEN:
      Because it is more .....
   The *NEXT* word in the rewritten sentence is

   A. subtly   B. interesting   C. melodramatic
   D. used   E. hidden

4. Shaw's response to this is to withdraw, partially, from his public concerns into a more personal, private, and poetic form of expression.
   REWRITTEN:
      Shaw responded to this with a .... .
   Somewhere in the part of the rewritten sentence indicated by dots is the word

   A. partially   B. is to   C. withdraws
   D. publicly   E. withdrawal

5. But life draws him back again, against his will, in the form of uncontrollable instinct.
   REWRITTEN:
      He is ...
   The NEXT word in the rewritten sentence is

   A. uncontrollable   B. instinctive   C. back
   D. drawn   E. willful

6. Such destructive criticism accounts, in part, for the unpopularity of this drama, for the modern world wants affirmations.
   REWRITTEN:
      This drama is ....
   The NEXT word in the rewritten sentence is

   A. unpopular   B. accounted   C. criticized
   D. in part   E. destructive

7. Shaw is just as unable to accept the concept of a malevolent or determined man as to accept the concept of a determined and mindless universe.
   REWRITTEN:
      It is equally difficult ...
   Somewhere in the part of the rewritten sentence indicated by dots is (are) the word(s)

   A. unable   B. for him   C. just
   D. to conceive E. to understand

8. We know from his descriptions that Leeuwenhoek saw both plant and animal microorganisms and that among them may have been some bacteria.
   REWRITTEN:
      Among the plant and animal microorganisms which we ...
   The NEXT word in the rewritten sentence is

   A. saw   B. described   C. know
   D. assume   E. discovered

9. The Japanese quickly overcame the Russian fleet and then landed troops on the mainland of Asia.
   REWRITTEN:
      The Russian fleet ... .
   Somewhere in the part of the rewritten sentence indicated by dots is(are) the word(s)

   A. overcame   B. and then   C. defeated
   D. retreated E. who

10. Napoleon would not tolerate such an arrangement and sent an army of twenty thousand men to suppress the movement.
    REWRITTEN:
       The movement .....
    The NEXT word in the rewritten sentence is

    A. was   B. suppressed   C. would
    D. sent   E. of

11. To have the program succeed, Marx realized he would need the united support of work-   11._____
    ingmen all over the world.
    REWRITTEN:
        Marx realized that the success .....
    Somewhere in the part of the rewritten sentence indicated by dots is the word

    A. he   B. would   C. have
    D. required   E. to

12. His beautiful descriptions of nature reflect the poet's deep belief in the closeness of   12._____
    nature to the human soul.
    REWRITTEN:
        One reflection of .....
    The NEXT word(s) in the rewritten sentence is(are)

    A. beauty   B. the poet's   C. poetry
    D. the descriptions   E. closeness

13. The extraordinary play is a chronicle of O'Neill's own spiritual metamorphosis from a   13._____
    messianic into an existential rebel.
    REWRITTEN:
        O'Neill had undergone .....
    The NEXT word in the rewritten sentence is

    A. extraordinary   B. existentialism   C. rebelliousness
    D. spirituality   E. a

14. Considering its great influence, Europe is surprisingly small.   14._____
    REWRITTEN:
        The smallness of Europe is surprising when one ...
    The NEXT word in the rewritten sentence is

    A. influences   B. is   C. considers
    D. knows   E. consideration

15. Until late in the 1800's we knew nothing of a remarkable civilization which was old when   15._____
    the Greeks arrived.
    REWRITTEN:
        One remarkable civilization which was old when the Greeks arrived .....
    Somewhere in the part of the rewritten sentence indicated by dots is the word

    A. we   B. unknown   C. knew
    D. nothing E. of

16. Our knowledge of Aegean civilization comes largely from the work of two men.   16._____
    REWRITTEN:
        The work of two men ....
    The NEXT word in the rewritten sentence is

    A. comes   B. teaches   C. acknowledges
    D. enhances   E. contributes

17. Twelve of the most important deities formed a council, which was supposed to meet on snowcapped Mount Olympus, in northern Thessaly.
    REWRITTEN:
    Mount Olympus, in northern Thessaly, was supposed to be the..........
    The NEXT word(s) in the rewritten sentence is (are)

    A. meeting place   B. council   C. most important
    D. epitome   E. deities

18. In the United States the states and local governments regulate the public schools and supply them with funds.
    REWRITTEN:
    Public schools in the United States are .....
    Somewhere in the part of the rewritten sentence indicated by dots is the word

    A. them   B. regulate   C. subsidized
    D. governed   E. supplied

19. The obstacle of distance was partly overcome by the invention of the steamship and the building of the Suez Canal.
    REWRITTEN:
    The invention of the steamship and the building of the Suez Canal helped
    Somewhere in the part of the rewritten sentence indicated by dots is the word

    A. was   B. overcoming   C. overcome
    D. partly   E. shorten

20. Although cotton has been used for cloth since ancient times, It was not known in England until the seventeenth century when the East India Company brought *calico* (named for Calicut) from India.
    REWRITTEN:
    When the East India Company brought *calico* (named for Calicut) from India in the seventeenth century, it was England's first .....
    Somewhere in the part of the rewritten sentence indicated by dots is the word

    A. known   B. knowledge   C. was
    D. although   E. until

21. In the eighteenth century weaving was still done on the hand loom.
    REWRITTEN:
    The hand loom .....
    Somewhere in the part of the rewritten sentence indicated by dots is the word

    A. done   B. on   C. for
    D. remained   E. weaves

22. When rubbed with wool, amber accumulates a charge of static electricity and will then attract small pieces of pith or paper.
    REWRITTEN:
    Small pieces of pith or paper can .....
    The NEXT word in the rewritten sentence is

    A. accumulate   B. be   C. attract
    D. charge   E. then

23. As a result of the Second World War, cities were devastated and millions were left homeless.
   REWRITTEN:
   The Second World War resulted .....
   Somewhere in the part of the rewritten sentence indicated by dots is the word

   A. leaving   B. devastating   C. were
   D. deprivation   E. devastated

24. With the growing urbanization and mechanization of modern life has come increasing recognition of the evils of drunkenness.
   REWRITTEN:
   The evils of drunkenness have become .....
   Somewhere in the part of the rewritten sentence indicated by dots is the word

   A. recognition   B. recognized   C. come
   D. increasing   E. increased

25. Chekhov dilutes the melodramatic pathos by qualifying our sympathy for the victims.
   REWRITTEN:
   The result of Chekhov's .....
   The NEXT word in the rewritten sentence is

   A. dilution   B. diluting   C. melodramatic
   D. qualification   E. qualifying

KEYS (CORRECT ANSWERS)

1.	C	11.	D
2.	B	12.	B
3.	A	13.	E
4.	E	14.	C
5.	D	15.	B
6.	A	16.	E
7.	B	17.	A
8.	C	18.	E
9.	E	19.	C
10.	A	20.	D

21.	C
22.	B
23.	A
24.	B
25.	E

6 (#1)

ACCEPTABLY REWRITTEN

1. Because its central figure conforms to the definitions of the mythic hero supplied by Northrup Frye, in THE ANATOMY OF CRITICISM, the messianic drama is <u>categorized</u> in the literary genre of myth or romance.

2. Julian is revealed <u>by</u> Ibsen to be a false Messiah, in THE EMPEROR JULIAN, the second part of the drama.

3. Because it is more <u>subtly</u> hidden, Chekhov's use of melodrama is more interesting.

4. Shaw responded to this with a partial <u>withdrawal</u> from his public concerns into a more personal, private, and, poetic form of expression.

5. He is <u>drawn</u> back again by life, against his will, in the form of uncontrollable instinct.

6. This drama is <u>unpopular</u> partly because it receives such destructive criticism when the modern world wants affirmations.

7. It is equally difficult for Shaw to accept the concept of a malevolent or determined man as it is <u>for him</u> to accept the concept of a determined and mindless universe.

8. Among the plant and animal microrganisms which we <u>know</u> that Leewen-hoek saw because of his descriptions, there may have been some bacteria.

9. The Russian fleet was quickly overcome by the Japanese <u>who</u> then landed troops on the mainland of Asia.

10. The movement <u>was</u> suppressed by an army of twenty thousand men sent by Napoleon who would not tolerate such an arrangement.

11. Marx realized that the success of the program <u>required</u> the united support of workingmen all over the world.

12. One reflection of <u>the poet's</u> deep belief in the closeness of nature to the human soul can be found in his beautiful descriptions of nature.

13. O'Neill had undergone <u>a</u> spiritual metamorphosis from a messianic into an existential rebel, of which this play is an extraordinary chronicle.

14. The smallness of Europe is surprising when one <u>considers</u> its great influence.

15. One remarkable civilization which was old when the Greeks arrived was <u>unknown</u> to us until late in the 1800's.

16. The work of two men <u>contributes</u> largely to our knowledge of Aegean civilization.

17. Snowcapped Mount Olympus, in northern Thessaly, was supposed to be the <u>meeting place</u> for a council formed by twelve of the most important deities.

18. Public schools in the United States are regulated and <u>supplied</u> with funds by the states and local government.

19. The invention of the steamship and the building of the Suez Canal helped to <u>overcome</u> the obstacle of distance.

20. When the East India Company brought *calico* (named for Calicut) from India in the seventeenth century, it was England's first introduction to cotton, <u>although</u> it has been used for cloth since ancient times.

21. The hand loom was still used <u>for</u> weaving in the eighteenth century.

22. Small pieces of pith or paper can <u>be</u> attracted by amber if it has been rubbed with wool to accumulate a charge of static electricity.

23. The Second World War resulted in the devastation of cities and the <u>leaving</u> homeless of millions.

24. The evils of drunkenness have become increasingly <u>recognized</u> with the growing urbanization and mechanization of modern life.

25. The result of Chekhov's <u>qualifying</u> our sympathy for the victims is the dilution of the melodramatic pathos.

TEST 2

1. While gazing through his microscope at a drop of water, he saw many kinds of creatures with one or a few cells, which wriggled about and devoured food.
   BEGIN THE SENTENCE WITH
   　　Many kinds of creatures with one or a few cells wriggling about .....
   Somewhere in the part of the rewritten sentence indicated by dots is (are) the word(s)

   A. he saw   B. and devoured   C. which
   D. by him   E. while gazing

2. The worship of ancestors in China must have arisen in prehistoric times, judging from the reference to it in the most ancient Chinese literature.
   SUBSTITUTE
   　　..........since the most ancient Chinese literature for judging ...
   The NEXT words in the rewritten sentence are

   A. the references   B. is judged   C. refers it
   D. refers to   E. from the

3. She divided the bread among them, without considering a share for herself.
   BEGIN THE SENTENCE WITH
   　　She did not .....
   Somewhere in the part of the rewritten sentence indicated by dots is(are) the word(s)

   A. divided   B. when she   C. without
   D. considering   E. dividing

4. Since Smith has been a resident here for twenty years, we should give serious consideration to his suggestions.
   SUBSTITUTE
   　　... seriously for give serious
   THE NEXT WORD(S) IN THE REWRITTEN SENTENCE IS (ARE)

   A. to   B. consideration   C. consider
   D. give consideration E. would

5. In the fight for women's suffrage one judge's decision had little effect, for the most part, upon the ladies' determination.
   CHANGE
   　　...effect to effected
   Somewhere in the part of the rewritten sentence indicated by dots is (are) the word(s)

   A. had   B. upon   C. part, upon
   D. had, for   E. part, very little

6. His approach to the committee was certainly not conducive to a cordial reception of his proposals, which were, at best, of doubtful validity.
   BEGIN THE SENTENCE WITH
   　　He approached .....
   Somewhere in the part of the rewritten sentence Indicated by dots is(are) the word(s)

   A. was certainly   B. which was   C. to the
   D. his   E. committee was

7. When the thirsty horse had drunk its fill, it trotted briskly down the road.
   BEGIN THE SENTENCE WITH
       The thirsty horse ......
   The NEXT word(s) in the rewritten sentence is (are)

   A. having   B. it trotted   C. when
   D. had   E. had trotted

8. This country must either set up flood controls or be prepared to lose billions of dollars annually.
   BEGIN THE SENTENCE WITH
       If......
   Somewhere in the part of the rewritten sentence indicated by dots is (are) the word(s)

   A. either   B. must set   C. does not
   D. or   E. country must

9. They are not in Boston now, but I think they're going to that city next week.
   BEGIN THE SENTENCE WITH
       I think .....
   Somewhere in the part of the rewritten sentence indicated by dots is (are) the word(s)

   A. but I   B. in Boston   C. to Boston
   D. to that   E. now, but

10. Mt.Kinley, in Alaska, is higher than any other mountain in North America.
    INSERT THE WORD
        <u>the</u> after <u>is</u> .....
    The NEXT word in the rewritten sentence is

    A. highest   B. other   C. any
    D. than   E. higher

11. As a result of the Industrial Revolution, cities grew very rapidly and the demand for food and raw materials increased.
    BEGIN THE SENTENCE WITH
        A result .....
    Somewhere in the part of the rewritten sentence indicated by dots is (are) the word(s)

    A. grew   B. rapidly   C. the demand
    D. materials increased   E. increased demand

12. Since the late eighteenth century, when the American and French revolutions took place, democracy has had a slow but persistent growth.
    SUBSTITUTE
        <u>After</u> for <u>Since</u> .....
    Somewhere in the part of the rewritten sentence indicated by dots is (are) the word(s)

    A. slow   B. has had   C. persistently
    D. growth   E. slow but persistent

13. The Treaty of Versailles placed the entire blame for World War I on Germany and her allies.
    BEGIN THE SENTENCE WITH
        Germany......
    Somewhere in the part of the rewritten sentence indicated by dots is the word

	A. placed	B. on	C. blame
	D. were	E. entire	

14. A few years after Harvey's death, other scientists began to study the blood vessels with the aid of microscopes. 14.___
    BEGIN THE SENTENCE WITH
      Blood vessels .....
    Somewhere in the part of the rewritten sentence indicated by dots is (are) the word(s)

    A. by   B. began   C. study
    D. to   E. the study

15. This pamphlet is in response to requests of various groups for a more permanent and usable form of this material. 15.___
    BEGIN THE SENTENCE WITH
      To provide .....
    Somewhere in the part of the rewritten sentence indicated by dots is (are) the word(s)

    A. responding to   B. as a response to   C. requested
    D. in response to   E. requesting

16. The space science events chosen for development illustrate types of experiences in which mathematics and science have a mutually enhancing effect on each other. 16.___
    SUBSTITUTE
      ...are illustrated by for illustrate...
    Somewhere in the part of the rewritten sentence indicated by dots is(are) the word(s)

    A. have had   B. have   C. had had
    D. may be shown to have E. has

17. The criteria will be useful throughout the course in setting up specific objectives, providing learning experiences, and making periodic evaluations. 17.___
    SUBSTITUTE
      Use the criteria throughout the course for The criteria will be useful throughout the course ...
    The NEXT word in the rewritten sentence is

    A. in   B. for   C. to   D. with   E. by

18. The objectives of a training program are achieved by learning experiences designed to help the trainees develop those behaviors and abilities designated in the objectives. 18.___
    BEGIN THE SENTENCE WITH
      To achieve .....
    Somewhere in the part of the rewritten sentence indicated by dots is (are) the word(s)

    A. employ   B. to use   C. it will be useful
    D. create   E. to create

19. Because all of the suggested facilities will not be available in every community, it remains for the teacher to modify or supplement the following suggestions. 19.___
    BEGIN THE SENTENCE WITH
      The teacher .....
    The word that occurs IMMEDIATELY before the word modify, is

    A. could   B. might   C. would   D. must   E. should

20. Although teachers differ in their ways or organizing and coordinating important parts of their presentations, they agree that the purpose of a lesson is effective and meaningful classroom instruction.
BEGIN THE SENTENCE WITH
    Although teachers agree .....
The FIRST word of the main clause in the rewritten sentence is

    A. the   B. teachers   C. they   D. differing   E. it

21. Many common physical quantities such as temperature, the speed of a moving object, or the displacement of a ship can be expressed as a certain number of units.
BEGIN THE SENTENCE WITH
    One can express .....
The NEXT word(s) in the rewritten sentence is (are)

    A. as   B. many   C. in   D. a ship's   E. the

22. A parallel-tuned circuit, on the other hand, offers a very high impedance to currents of its natural, or resonant, frequency and a relatively low impedance to others.
BEGIN THE SENTENCE WITH
    A very high impedance .....
The NEXT words in the rewritten sentence are

    A. is offered to   B. offers to   C. is offered for
    D. is offered by   E. on the other hand

23. As the term implies, a voltage feedback amplifier transfers a voltage from the output of the amplifier back to its input.
CHANGE
    ... transfers to is transferred ...
The FIRST words of the rewritten sentence are

    A. A voltage
    B. Back to its input
    C. A voltage feedback amplifier
    D. In accordance with the term
    E. From the output

24. Unemployment among youth is a serious problem now, and unless the economy grows much more rapidly in the future than it has during the past decade, today's youngsters will feel the sharp pinch of declining ratios of new employment opportunities to persons seeking work.
BEGIN THE SENTENCE WITH
    Unless the economy grows, ...
The LAST CLAUSE in the rewritten sentence begins with

    A. today's   B. unemployment   C. and unless
    D. now   E. since

25. In a great society, talents are evoked and realized, creative minds probe the frontiers of knowledge, expectations of excellence are widely shared.
BEGIN THE SENTENCE WITH
    A great society .....
The NEXT words in the rewritten sentence are

A. evokes and realizes
B. talents, creative minds, and expectations of excellence
C. features
D. is characterized by
E. is one in which

KEYS (CORRECT ANSWERS)

1. D
2. D
3. B
4. C
5. E

6. B
7. A
8. C
9. C
10. A

11. E
12. C
13. D
14. A
15. D

16. B
17. C
18. A
19. E
20. C

21. A
22. E
23. A
24. E
25. E

ACCEPTABLY REWRITTEN

1. Many kinds of creatures with one or a few cells, wriggling about and devouring food, were seen <u>by him</u> while he was gazing through his microscope at a drop of water.

2. The worship of ancestors in China must have arisen in prehistoric times since the most ancient Chinese literature <u>refers to</u> it.

3. She did not consider a share for herself <u>when she</u> divided the bread among them.

4. Since Smith has been a resident here for twenty years, we should seriously <u>consider</u> his suggestions.

5. In the fight for women's suffrage one judge's decision affected the ladies' decision, for the most <u>part, very little.</u>

6 (#2)

6. He approached the committee in a way which was certainly not conducive to a cordial reception of his proposals, which were, at best, of doubtful validity.

7. The thirsty horse, having drunk its fill, trotted briskly down the road.

8. If this country does not set up flood controls, it must be prepared to lose billions of dollars annually.

9. I think they're going to Boston next week, though they're not in that city now.

10. Mt.Kinley, in Alaska, is the highest mountain in North America.

11. A result of the Industrial Revolution was the very rapid growth of cities and the increased demand for food and raw materials.

12. After the late eighteenth century, when the American and French revolutions took place, democracy grew slowly, but persistently.

13. Germany and her allies were blamed entirely for World War I by the Treaty of Versailles.

14. Blood vessels were studied by other scientists, with the aid of microscopes, a few years after Harvey's death.

15. To provide a more permanent and usable form of this material, in response to the requests of various groups, this pamphlet has been written.

16. The space science events chosen for development are illustrated by types of experiences in which mathematics and science have a mutually enhancing effect on each other.

17. Use the criteria throughout the course to set up specific objectives, provide learning experiences, and make periodic evaluations.

18. To achieve the objectives of a training program employ learning experiences designed to help the trainees develop those behaviors and abilities designated in the objectives.

19. The teacher should modify or supplement the following suggestions because all of the suggested facilities will not be available in every community.

20. Although teachers agree that the purpose of a lesson is effective and meaningful classroom instruction, they differ in their ways of organizing and coordinating important parts of their presentations.

21. One can express as a certain number of units many common physical quantities such as temperature, the speed of a moving object, or the displacement of a ship.

22. A very high impedance, on the other hand, is offered by a parallel-tuned circuit to currents of its natural, or resonant, frequency and a relatively low impedance to others.

23. A voltage is transferred from the output of the amplifier back to its input by a voltage feedback amplifier, as its name implies.

24. Unless the economy grows much more rapidly in the future than it has during the past decade, today's youngsters will feel the sharp pinch of declining ratios of new employment opportunities to persons seeking work <u>since</u> unemployment among youth is a serious problem now.

25. A great society <u>is one in which</u> talents are evoked and realized, creative minds probe the frontiers of knowledge, expectations of excellence are widely shared.

BASIC FUNDAMENTALS OF WRITTEN COMMUNICATION

CONTENTS	Page
INSTRUCTIONAL OBJECTIVES	1
CONTENT	1
Introduction	1
1. Business Writing	1
Letters	
Selet the letter type	
Select the Right Format	
Know the Letter Elements	
Be Breef	
Use Concrete Nouns	
Use Active Verbs	
Use a Natural Tone	
Forms	4
Memoranda	5
Minutes of meetings	5
Short Reports	6
News Releases	8
2. Reporting on a Topic	9
Preparation for the Report	9
What is the Purpose of the Report?	
What Questions Should it Answer?	
Where Can the Relevant information be obtained?	
The Text of the Report	10
What Are the Answers to the Questions?	
Organizing the Report	
The Writer's Responsibilities	11
Conclusions and Recommendations	11
3. Persuasive Writing	11
General Guidelines for Writing	11
Persuasively	
Know the Source Credibility	
Avoid Overemotional Appeal	
Consider the Other Man's Point of wiew	
Interpersonal Communications	12
Conditions of Persuading	
The Persuassion campain	
4. Instructional Writing	13
Advances Organizers	
Practice	
Errorless Learning	
Feedback	
STUDENT LEARNING ACTIVITIES	16
TEACHERS MANAGEMENT ACTIVTIES	17
EVALUATION QUESTIONS	19

BASIC FUNDAMENTALS OF WRITTEN COMMUNICATION

INSTRUCTIONAL OBJECTIVES

1. Ability to write legibly.
2. Ability to fill out forms and applications correctly.
3. Ability to take messages and notes accurately.
4. Ability to write letters effectively.
5. Ability to write directions and instructions clearly.
6. Ability to outline written and spoken information.
7. Ability to persuade or teach others through written communication.
8. Ability to write effective overviews and summaries.
9. Ability to make smooth transitions within written communications.
10. Ability to use language forms appropriate for the reader.
11. Ability to prepare effective informational reports.

CONTENT

INTRODUCTION

Public-service employees are required to prepare written communications for a variety of purposes. Written communication is a fundamental tool, not only for the public-service occupations, but throughout the world of work. Many public-service occupations require written communication with ordinary citizens of diverse backgrounds, so the trainee should develop the ability to write in simple, nontechnical language that the ordinary citizen will understand.

This unit is designed to develop the student's ability to communicate effectively in writing for a number of different purposes and in a number of different formats. Whatever the particular purpose or format, how-- ever, effective writing will require the writer:

- to have a clear idea of his purpose and his audience;
- to organize his thoughts and information in an orderly way;
- to express himself concisely, accurately, and concretely;
- to report relevant facts;
- to explain and summarize ideas clearly; and
- to evaluate the effectiveness of his communication.

1. BUSINESS WRITING

    Several forms of written communication tend to recur frequently in most public-service agencies, including:
    - letters
    - forms
    - memoranda
    - minutes of meetings
    - short reports
    - telegrams and cables
    - news releases
    - and many others

    The public-service employee should be familiar with the principles of writing in these forms, and should be able to apply them in preparing effective communications.

    Letters

    Every letter sent from a public-service agency should be considered an ambassador of goodwill. The impression it creates may mean the difference between favorable public attitudes or unfavorable ones. It may mean the difference between creating a friend or an enemy for the agency. Every public-service employee has a responsibility to serve the public effectively and to provide services in an efficient and courteous manner. The letters an agency sends out reflect its attitudes toward the public.

The impression a letter creates depends upon both its appearance and its tone. A letter which shows erasures and pen written corrections gives an impression that the sending agency is slovenly. Similarly, a rude or impersonal letter creates the impression that the agency is insensitive or unfeeling. In preparing letters, the employee should apply principles of style and tone which will serve to create the most favorable impression.

Select the Letter Type. The two most common types of business letters are letters of inquiry and letters of response - that is, "asking" letters and "answering" letters. Whichever type of letter the employee is asked to write, the following guidelines will simplify the task and help to achieve a style and tone which will create a favorable impression on the reader.

Select the Right Format. Several styles of letter format are in common use today, including:

- the indented format,
- the block format, and
- the semi-block format.

Modified forms of these are also in use in some offices. The student should become familiar with the formats preferred for usage in his office, and be able to use whichever form the employer requests.

Know the Letter Elements. Every letter includes certain basic elements, such as:

- the letterhead, which identifies the name and address of the sender.
- the date on which the letter was transmitted.
- the inside address, with the name, street, city, and state of the addressee.
- the salutation, greeting the addressee.
- the body, containing the message.
- the complimentary close, the "good-bye" of the business letter.
- the signature, handwritten by the sender.
- the typed signature, the typewritten name and title of the sender.

In addition, several other elements are occasionally found in business letters:

- the *attention line,* directing the letter to the attention of a particular individual or his representative.
- the *subject line,* informing the reader at a glance of the subject of the letter.

- the *enclosure notation,* noting items enclosed with the letter.
- the *copy notation,* listing other persons who receive copies of the letter.
- the *postscript,* an afterthought sometimes (but not normally) added following the last typed line of the letter.

Be *Brief.* Use only the words which help to say what is needed in a clear and straightforward manner. Do not repeat information already known to the reader, or contained elsewhere in the letter. Likewise, do not repeat information contained in the letter being answered. Rather than repeat the content of a previous letter, one can say something like, "Please refer to our letter dated March 5:"

An employee can shorten his letters by using single words that serve the same function as longer phrases. Many commonly used phrases can be replaced by single words. For example,

Phrase	Single word
in order to	to
in reference to in	about
the amount of	for, of
in a number of cases	some
in view of	because
with regard to	about, in

Similarly, avoid the use of adjectives and nouns that are formed from verbs. If the root verbs are used instead, the writing will be more concise and more vivid. For example,

Noun form	Verb form
We made an adjustment on our books	We adjusted our books
We are sorry we cannot make a replacement of	We are sorry we cannot replace
Please make a correction in our order	Please correct our order

Be on the lookout for unnecessary adjectives and adverbs which tend to clutter letters without adding information or improving style. Such unnecessary words tend to distract the reader and make it more difficult for him to grasp the main points. Observe how the superfluous words, italicized in the following example, obscure the meaning: "You may be *very much* disappointed to learn that the *excessively large* demand for our *highly popular recent* publication, 'Your Income Taxes,' has led to an *unexpected* shortage of this *attractive* publication and we *sadly* expect they will not be replenished until *quite* late this year."

Summarizing, then, a *good letter is simple and clear, with short, simple words, sentences, and paragraphs. Related parts* of *sentences and paragraphs are kept together and placed in an order which makes it easy for the reader to follow the main thoughts.*

<u>Be Natural</u>. Whenever possible, use a human touch. Use names and personal pronouns to let the reader know the letter was written by a person, not an institution. Instead of saying, "It is the policy of this agency to contact its clients once each year to confirm their status," try this: "Our policy, Mr. Jones, is to confirm your status once each year."

<u>Use Concrete Nouns</u>. Avoid using abstract words and generalizations. Use names of objects, places, and persons rather than abstractions.

<u>Use Active verbs</u>. The passive voice gives a motionless, weak tone to most writing. Instead of "The minutes were taken by Mrs. Smith," say, "Mrs. Smith took the minutes." Instead of "The plans were prepared by the banquet committee," say, "The banquet committee prepared the plans."

<u>Use a Natural Tone</u>. Many people tend to become hard, cold, and unnatural the moment they write a letter. *Communicating by letter should have the same natural tone of conversation used in everyday speech.* One way to achieve a natural and personal tone in the majority of letters is through the use of personal pronouns. Instead of saying, "Referring to your letter of March 5, reporting the non-receipt of goods ordered last February 15, please be advised that the goods were shipped as requested," say, "I am sorry to hear that you failed to receive the items you ordered last February 15. We shipped them the same day we received your letter."

<u>Forms</u>

In most businesses and public service agencies, repetitive work is simplified by the use of *forms*. Forms exist for nearly every purpose imaginable: for ordering supplies, preparing invoices, applying for jobs, applying for insurance, paying taxes, recording inventories, and so on. While the forms encountered in different agencies may differ widely, several principles should be applied in completing any form:

- <u>Legibility</u>. Entries on forms should be clear and legible. Print or type wherever possible. When space provided is insufficient, attach a supplementary sheet to the form.

- <u>Completeness</u>. Make an entry in every space provided on the form. If a particular space does not apply to the applicant, enter there the term "N/A" (for "not applicable"). The reader of the completed form will then know that the applicant did not simply overlook that space.

- <u>Conciseness</u>. Forms are intended to elicit a maximum amount of information in the least possible space. When completing a form, it is usually not necessary to write complete sentences. Provide the necessary information in the least possible words.

- *Accuracy.* Be sure the information provided on the form is accurate. If the entry is a number, such as a social security number or an address, double-check the correctness of the number. Be sure of the spelling of names, No one appreciates receiving a communication in which his name is misspelled.

Memoranda

The written communications passing between offices or departments are usually transmitted in a form known as *"interoffice memorandum."* The headings most often used on such "memos" are:

- TO: identifying the addressee,
- FROM: identifying the sender or the originating office,
- SUBJECT: identifying briefly the subject of the memo,
- DATE: identifying the date the memo was prepared.

Larger agencies may also use headings such as FILE or REFERENCE NO. to aid in filing and retrieving memoranda.

In writing a memo, many of the same rules for letter-writing may be applied. Both the appearance and tone of the memo should create a pleasing impression. The format should be neat and follow the standards set by the originating office. The tone should be friendly, courteous, and considerate. The language should be clear, concise, and complete.

Memos usually dispense with salutations, complimentary closings, and signatures of the writers. In most other respects, however, the memorandum will follow the rules of good letter-writing.

Minutes of Meetings

Most formal public-service organization conduct meetings from time to time at which group decisions are made about agency policies, procedures, and work assignments. The records of such meetings are called *minutes.*

Minutes should be written as clearly and simply as possible, summarizing only the essential facts and decisions made at the meeting. While some issue may have been discussed at great length, only the final decision or resolution made of it should be recorded in the minutes. Information of this sort is usually included:

- Time and place of the call to order,
- Presiding officer and secretary,
- Voting members present (with names, if a small organization),

- Approval and corrections of previous minutes,
- Urgent business,
- Old business,
- New business,
- Time of adjournment,
- Signature of recorder.

Minutes should be written in a factual and objective style. The opinions of the recorder should not be in evidence. Every item of business coming up before a meeting should be included in the minutes, together with its disposition. For example:

- "M/S/P (Moved, seconded, passed) that Mr. Thomas Jones take responsibility for rewriting the personnel procedures manual."
- "Discussion of the summer vacation schedule was tabled until the next meeting."
- "M/S/P, a resolution that no client of the agency should be kept waiting more than 20 minutes for an interview."

Note that considerable discussion may have surrounded each of the above items in the minutes, but that only the topic and its resolution are recorded.

Short Reports

The public-service employee often is called upon to prepare a short report gathering and interpreting information on a single topic. Reports of this kind are sometimes prepared so that all the relevant information may be assembled in one place to aid the organization in making certain decisions. Such reports may be read primarily by the staff of the organization or by others closely related to the decision-making process.

Reports may be prepared at other times for distribution to the public or to other agencies and institutions. These reports may serve the purpose of informing public opinion or persuading others on matters of public policy.

Whatever the purpose of the short report, its physical appearance and style of presentation should be designed to create a favorable impression on the reader. Even if the report is distributed only within the writer's own unit, an attractive, clear, thorough report will reflect the writer's dedication to his assignment and the pride he takes in his work.

Some guidelines which will assist the trainee in preparation of effective short reports include use of the following:

- A good quality paper;
- Wide and even margins, allowing binding room;

- An accepted standard style of typing;
- A title page;
- A table of contents (for more lengthy reports only);
- A graphic numbering or outlining system, if needed for clarity;
- Graphics and photos to clarify meaning when useful;
- Footnotes, used sparingly, and only when they contribute to the report;
- A bibliography of sources, using a standard citation style.

A discussion of the organization of content for informational reports follows later in this document.

News Releases

From time to time, the public-service employees may be called upon to prepare a news release for his agency. Whenever the activities of the agency are newsworthy or of interest to the public, the agency has an obligation to report such activities to the press. The most common means for such reporting is by using the press release. Most newspapers and broadcasting stations are initially informed of agencies' activities by news releases distributed by the agencies themselves. Thus, the news release is a basic tool for communicating with the public served by the agency.

The news release is written in news style, with these basic characteristics:

- Sentences are short and simple.

- Paragraphs are short (one or two sentences) and relate to a single item of information.

- Paragraphs are arranged in *inverted order*—the most important in information appears first.

- The first or *lead* paragraph summarizes the entire story. If the reader went no further, he would have the essential information.

- Subsequent paragraphs provide further details, the most important occurring first.

- Reported information is attributed to sources; that is, the source of the news is reported in the story.

- The expression of the writer's opinions is scrupulously avoided.

- The 5 W's (who, what, why, where, when) are included.

News releases should be typed double spaced on standard 8 1/2 x 11 paper, with generous margins and at least 2" of open space above the lead paragraph. Do not write headlines - that is the editor's job. At the top of the first page of the release include the name of the agency releasing the story and the name and phone number of the person to contact if more information is needed. If the release runs more than one page, end each page with the word "-more-" to indicate that more copy follows. End the release with the symbols "###" to indicate that the copy ends at that point.

Accuracy and physical appearance are essential characteristics of the news release. Typographical errors, or errors of fact, such as misspelled names, lead editors to doubt the reliability of the story. Great care should be taken to assure the accuracy and reliability of a news release.

2. REPORTING ON A TOPIC

At one time or another, most public-service employees will be asked to prepare a report on some topic. Usually the need for the report grows out of some policy decision contemplated by the agency for which full information must be considered. For example:

- Should the agency undertake some new project or service?
- Should working conditions be changed?
- Are new specialists needed on the staff?
- Or should a branch office be opened up?

Or any of a hundred other such decisions which the agency must make from time to time.

When called upon to prepare such a report, the employee should have a model to follow which will guide his collection of information and will help him to prepare an effective and useful report.

As with other forms of written communication, both the physical appearance and content of the report are important to create a favorable impression and to engender confidence. The physical appearance of such reports has been discussed earlier; additional suggestions for reports are given in Unit 3. Basic guidelines follow below for organizing and preparing the content.

Preparation for the Report

What is the Purpose of the Report? The preparer of the report should have clearly in mind why the report is needed:

- What is the decision being contemplated by the agency?
- To what use will the report be put?

Before beginning to prepare the report, the writer should discuss its purpose fully with the decision-making staff to articulate the purpose the report is intended to serve. If the employee is himself initiating the report, it would be well to discuss its purpose with colleagues to assure that its purpose is clear in his own mind.

What Questions Should the Report Answer? Once the purpose of the report is clear, the questions the report must answer may begin to become clear. For example, if the decision faced by the agency is whether or not to offer a new service, questions may be asked such as these:

- What persons would be served by the new service?

- What would the new service cost?
- What new staff would be needed?
- What new equipment and facilities would be needed?
- What alternative ways exist for offering the service?
- How might the new service be administered?

And so on. Unless the purpose of the report is clear, it is difficult to decide what specific questions need to be answered. Once the purpose is clear, these questions can be specified.

<u>Where Can the Relevant Information be Obtained</u>? Once the questions are clear in the writer's mind, he can identify the information he will need to answer them. Information may usually be obtained from two general sources:

- *Relevant documents.* Records, publications, and other reports are often useful in locating the information needed to answer particular questions. These may be in the files of the writer's own agency, in other agencies, or in libraries.

- *Personal contacts.* Persons in a position to know the needed information may be contacted in person, by phone, or by letter. Such contacts are especially important in obtaining firsthand accounts of previous experience.

<u>The Text of the Report</u>

<u>What are the Answers to the Questions</u>? Once the relevant information is in hand, the answers to the questions may be assembled.

- What does the information reveal? This activity amounts to summarizing the information obtained. It often helps to organize this summary around the specific questions asked by the report. For example, if the report asks in one part, "What are the costs of the new service likely to be?" one section of the report should summarize the information gathered to answer this question.

<u>Organizing the Report.</u> The organization of a report into main and subsections depends upon the nature of the report. Reports will differ widely in their organization and treatment. In general, however, the report should generally follow the pattern previously discussed. That is, reports which generally include the following subjects in order will be found to be clear in their intent and to communicate effectively:

- *Description of problem or purpose.* Example: "One problem facing our agency is whether or not we should extend our hours of operation to better serve the public. This report is intended to examine the problem and make recommendations."

- *Questions to be answered.* Example: "In examining this problem, answers were sought to the following questions: What persons would be served? What would it cost? What staff would be needed?"

- *Information sources.* Example: "To answer these questions, letters of complaint for the past three years were examined. Interviews with clients were conducted by phone and in person, phone interviews were conducted with the agency directors in Memphis, Philadelphia, and Chicago."

- *Summary of findings.* Example: "At least 25 percent of the agency's clients would be served better by evening or Saturday service. The costs of operating eight hours of extended service would be negligible, since the service could be provided by rescheduling work assignments. The present staff report they would be inconvenienced by evening and Saturday work assignments."

<u>The Writer's Responsibilities.</u> It is the writer's responsibility to address finally the original purpose of the report. Once the questions have been answered, an informed judgment can be made as to the decision facing the agency. It is at this stage that the writer attempts to draw conclusions from the information he has gathered and summarized. For example, if the original purpose of the report was to help make a decision about whether or not the agency should offer a new service, the writer should draw conclusions from the information and recommend either for or against the new service.

<u>Conclusions and Recommendations.</u> Example: "It appears that operating during extended hours would better serve a significant number of clients. The writer recommends that the agency offer this new service. The present staff should be given temporary assignments to cover the extended hours. As new staff are hired to replace separating persons, they should be hired specifically to cover the extended hours."

3. <u>PERSUASIVE WRITING</u>

   Often in life, people are called upon to persuade individuals and groups to adopt ideas believed to be good, or attitudes favorable to ideas thought to be worthwhile or behavior believed to be beneficial. The public service employee may find he must persuade the staff of his own agency, his superiors, the clients of the agency, or the general public in his community.

   Persuading others by means of written and other forms of communication is a difficult task and requires much practice. Some principles have emerged from the study of persuasion which may provide some guidelines for developing a model for persuasive writing.

General Guidelines for Writing Persuasively

Know the Credibility of the Source. People are more likely to be persuaded by a message they perceive originates from a trustworthy source. Their trust is enhanced if the source is seen as authoritative, or knowledgeable on the issue discussed in the message. Their trust is increased also if the source appears to have nothing to gain either way, has no vested interest in the final decision. Then, the assertions made in persuasive writing should be backed up by referencing trustworthy and disinterested information sources.

Avoid Overemotional Appeals. Appealing to the common emotions of man—love, hate, fear, sex, etc.—can have a favorable effect on the outcome of a persuasive message. But care should be taken because, if the appeal is too strong, it can lead to a reverse effect. For example, if an agency wanted to persuade the public to get chest X-rays, it would have much greater chance of success if it adopted a positive and helpful attitude rather than trying to frighten them into this action. For instance, appealing mildly to the sense of well-being which accompanies knowledge of one's own good health, instead of shocking the public by showing horror pictures of patients who died from lack of timely X-rays.

Consider the Other Man's Point of View. To persuade another to one's own point of view, should the writer include information and arguments contrary to his own position? Or should he argue only for his own side?

Generally, it depends on where most of the audience stand in the first place. If most of the audience already favor the position being advocated, then the writer will probably do better including only information favorable to his position. However, if the greater part of the audience are likely to oppose this position, then the writer would probably be better off including their arguments also. In this case, he may be helping his cause by rebutting the opposing arguments as he introduces them into the writing.

An example of this technique might occur in arguing for such an idea as a four-day, forty-hour workweek. Thus: "Many people feel that the ten-hour day is too long and that they would arrive home too late for their regular dinner hour. But think! If you have dinner a littler later each night, you'll have a three-day weekend every week. More days free to go fishing, or camping. More days with your wife and children." That is good persuasive writing!

Interpersonal Communications

The important role of interpersonal communication in persuading others—face-to-face and person-to-person communications—has been well documented. Mass mailings or printed messages will likely have less effect than personal letters and conversations between persons already known to each other. In any persuasion campaign the personal touch is very important.

An individual in persuading a large number of persons will likely be more effective if he can organize a letter-writing campaign of persuasive messages written by persons favorable to his position to their friends and acquaintances, than if his campaign is based upon sending out a mass mailing of a printed message.

Conditions for Persuading. In order for an audience of one or many to be persuaded in the manner desired, these conditions must be met:

- the audience must be *exposed* to the message,
- members of the audience must *perceive* the intent of the message,
- they must *remember* the message afterwards,
- each member must *decide* whether or not to adopt the ideas.

Each member of the audience will respond to a message differently. While every person may receive the message, not everyone will read it. Even among those who read it, not everyone will perceive it in the same way. Some will remember it longer than others. Not everyone will decide to adopt the ideas. These effects are called *selective exposure, selective perception, selective retention,* and *selective decision.*

The Persuasion Campaign. How can one counteract these selective effects in persuading others? One thing that is known is that *people tend to be influenced by persuasive messages which they are already predisposed to accept.* This means a person is more likely to persuade people a little than to persuade them a lot.

In planning a persuasion campaign, therefore, the messages should be tailored to the audiences. Success will be more likely if one starts with people who believe *almost* as the writer wants to persuade them to believe—people who are most likely to agree with the position advocated.

The writer also wants to use arguments based on values the particular audience already accepts. For example, in advocating a new teen-age job program, he might argue with business men that the program will help business; with parents, that it will build character; with teachers, that it is educational; with taxpayers, that it will reduce future taxes; and so on.

The idea is to find some way to make sure that each member of the particular audiences reached can see an advantage for himself, and for the writer to then tailor the messages for those audiences.

4. INSTRUCTIONAL WRITING

Another task that the public-service employee may expect to face from time to time is the instruction of some other person in the performance of a task. This may sometimes involve preparing written instructions to other employees in the unit, or preparing a training manual for new employees.

It may sometimes involve preparing instructional manuals for clients of the unit, such as "How to Apply for a Real Estate License," "How to Bathe your Baby," or "How to Recognize the Symptoms of Heart Disease."

Whatever the purpose or the audience, certain principles of instruction may be applied which will help make more effective these instructional or training communications. These are: *advance organizers, practice, errorless learning,* and *feedback.*

Advance Organizers

At or near the beginning of an instructional communication, it helps the learner if he is provided with what can be called an "advance organizer." This element of the communication performs two functions:

- it provides a framework or "map" for the leader to organize the information he will encounter,
- it helps the learner perceive his purpose in learning the tasks which will follow.

The first paragraphs in this section, for example, serve together as an advance organizer. The trainee is informed that he may be called upon to perform these tasks in his job *(perceived purpose),* and that he will be instructed in advance organizers, practice, errorless learning, and feedback *(framework, or "map").*

Practice

The notion of *practice makes perfect* is a sound instructional principle. When trying to teach someone to perform a task by means of written communication, the writer should build in many opportunities for practicing the task, or parts of it. This built-in practice should be both appropriate and active:

- *Appropriate practice* is practice which is directly related to learning the tasks at hand.

- *Active practice* is practice in actually performing the task at hand or parts of it, rather than simply reading about the task, or thinking about it.

By inserting questions into the text of the communication, by giving practice quizzes, exercises, or field work, one can build into his instructional communication the kind of practice necessary for the reader to readily learn the task.

Errorless Learning

The practice given learners should be easy to do. That is, they should not be asked to practice a task if they are likely to make a lot of mistakes. When a mistake is practiced it is likely to recur again and again, like spelling "demons," which have been spelled wrong so often it's difficult to recall the way they should be spelled. Because it is better to practice a task right from the first, it is important that learners do not make errors in practice.

- One method for encouraging correct practice is to give the reader hints, or *prompts,* to help him practice correctly.

- Another method is to instruct him in a logical sequence a little bit at a time. Don't try to teach everything at once. Break the task down into small parts and teach each part of the task in order. Then give the learner practice in each part of the task before giving him practice in the whole thing.

- A third way of encouraging errorless learning is to build in practice and review throughout the communication. The learner may forget part of the task if the teacher doesn't review it with him from time to time.

Remember, people primarily learn from what they do, so build in to the instructional communication many opportunities for the learner to practice correctly all of the parts of the task required for learning, first separately and then all together.

Feedback

The reader, or learner, can't judge how well he is learning the task unless he is informed of it. In a classroom situation, the teacher usually confirms that the learner has been successful, or points out the errors he made, and provides additional instruction. An instructional communication can also help learners in the same way, by providing *feedback* to the learner.

Following practice, the writer should include in his instructional communication information which will let the reader know whether he performed the task correctly. In case he didn't, the writer should also include some further information which will help the reader perform it correctly next time. This feedback, then, performs two functions:

- it helps the learner confirm that his practice was done correctly, and

- it helps him correct his performance of the task in case he made any errors.

Feedback will be most helpful to the learner if it occurs immediately following practice. The learner should be brought to know of his success or his errors just as soon as possible after practice.

STUDENT LEARNING ACTIVITIES

- Write "asking" and "answering" letters, and answer a letter of complaint, using the format assigned by the teacher.

- Write memoranda to other "offices" in a fictitious organization. Plan a field trip using only memos to communicate with other students in the class.

- Take minutes of a small group meeting. Or attend a meeting of the school board and take minutes.

- Write a short report on a public service occupation of special interest to you.

- Write a 15-word telegram reserving a single room at a hotel and asking to be picked up at the airport.

- Write a news release announcing a new service offered to the public by your agency.

- Based upon hearing a reading or pretaping of a report, summarize the report in news style.

- View films on effective communication, for example, *Getting the Facts, Words that Don't Inform,* and *A Message to No One.*

- For a given problem or purpose, compile a list of specific questions you would need to answer to write a report on the topic.

- For a given list of questions, discuss and compile a list of information sources relevant to the questions.

- As a member of a group, consider the problem of "What field trip should the class take to help students learn how to write an effective news release?" What questions will you need to answer? Where will you obtain your information?

- As a member of a group, gather the information and prepare a short report based on it for presentation to the class.

- Write a report on a problem assigned by your teacher.

- Write a brief persuasive letter to a friend on a given topic. Assume he does not already agree with you. Apply principles of source credibility, emotional appeals, and one or both sides of the issue to persuade him.

- Plan a persuasive campaign to persuade a given segment of your community to take some given action.

- Write a short instructional communication on a verbal learning task assigned by your teacher.

- Write a short instructional communication on a learning task which involves the operation of equipment.

- Try your instructional communications with a fellow student to check for errors during practice.

TEACHER MANAGEMENT ACTIVITIES

- Have students practice letter writing. Assign letters of "asking" and "answering." Read them a letter of complaint and ask them to write an answering letter. Establish common rules of format and style for each assignment. Change the rules from time to time to give practice in several styles.

- Have small groups plan an event, such as a field trip, assigning the various tasks to one another using only memoranda. Evaluate the effectiveness of each group's memo writing by the speed and completeness of their planning.

- Have the class attend a public meeting. Assign each the task of taking the minutes. Evaluate the minutes for brevity and completeness.

- Encourage each student to prepare a short report on a public service occupation of special interest to himself.

- Give the students practice in writing 15-word telegrams.

- Have the students prepare a news release announcing some new service offered to the public, such as "Taxpayers can now obtain help from the Internal Revenue Service in completing their income tax forms as a result of a new service now being offered by the agency."

- Give the students practice in summarizing and writing leads by giving them the facts of a news event and asking them to write a one or two-sentence lead summarizing the significant facts of the event.

- Read a speech or a story. Have students write a summary and a report of the speech or story in news style.

- Show films on effective communication, for example, *Getting the Facts, Words that Don't Inform,* and *A Message to No One.*

- State a general problem and have each student prepare a list of the specific questions implied by the problem.

- State a list of specific questions and discuss with the class the sources of information which might bear upon each of the questions.

- Have small groups consider and write short reports jointly on the general problem, "What field trip should the class take to help students learn how to write an effective news release?" Have each group identify the specific questions to be answered, with sources for needed information.

- Have each student identify and prepare a short report on a general problem of interest.

- Assign students to work in groups of three or four to draft a letter to a friend to persuade him to make a contribution to establish a new city art museum.

- Assign the students to groups of five or six, each group to map out a persuasive campaign on a given topic. Some topics are "Give Blood," "Get Chest X-Ray," "Quit Smoking," "Don't Litter," "Inspect Your House Wiring," etc.

- Have each student identify a simple verbal learning task and prepare an instructional communication to teach that task to another student not familiar with the task.

- Have each student prepare an instructional manual designed to train someone to operate some simple piece of equipment, such as an adding machine, a slide projector, a tape recorder, or something of similar complexity.

- Have each student try his instructional communication out on another student, unfamiliar with the task. He should observe the activities and responses of the trial student to identify errors made in practice. He should revise the communication, adding practice, review, and prompts wherever needed to reduce errors in practice.

EVALUATION QUESTIONS

Written Communications

1. Which type of letter would be correct for a public service worker to send?

    A. A letter containing erasures
    B. A letter reflecting goodwill
    C. A rude letter
    D. An impersonal letter

    1.____

2. Memos usually leave out:

    A. Complimentary closings
    B. The name of the sender
    C. The name of the addressee
    D. The date the memo was sent

    2.____

3. A good business letter would not contain:

    A. Short, simple words, sentences, and paragraphs
    B. Information contained in the letter being answered
    C. Concrete nouns and active verbs
    D. Orderly placed paragraphs

    3.____

4. In writing business letters it is important to:

    A. Use a conversational tone
    B. Use a hard, cold tone
    C. Use abstract words
    D. Use a passive tone

    4.____

5. Messages between departments in an agency are usually sent by:

    A. Letter
    B. Memo
    C. Telegram
    D. Long reports

    5.____

6. Repetitive work can be simplified by the use of:

    A. Memos
    B. Telegrams
    C. Forms
    D. Reports

    6.____

7. In filling out forms and applications, it is important to be:

    A. Legible
    B. Complete
    C. Accurate
    D. All of the above

    7.____

8. Memos should be: 8.___

    A. Clear
    B. Brief
    C. Complete
    D. All of the above

9. Minutes of meetings should not include: 9.___

    A. The opinions of the recorder
    B. The approval of previous minutes
    C. The corrections of previous minutes
    D. The voting members present

10. Reports are written by public service workers to: 10.___

    A. Assemble information in one place
    B. Aid the organization in making decisions
    C. Inform the public and other agencies
    D. All of the above

11. News releases should include: 11.___

    A. A lead paragraph summarizing the story
    B. Long paragraphs about many topics
    C. The writer's opinion
    D. All of the above

12. Readers of news releases and reports are influenced by the: 12.___

    A. Content of the material
    B. Accuracy of the material
    C. Physical appearance of the material
    D. All of the above

13. The contents of a report should include: 13.___

    A. A description of the problem
    B. The questions to be answered
    C. Unimportant information
    D. A summary of findings

14. People tend to be influenced easier if: 14.___

    A. They can see something in the position that would be advantageous to them
    B. They are almost ready to agree anyhow
    C. The appeal to the emotions is not overly strong
    D. All of the above

KEY (CORRECT ANSWERS)

1. B
2. A
3. B
4. A
5. B

6. C
7. D
8. D
9. A
10. D

11. A
12. D
13. C
14. D

www.ingramcontent.com/pod-product-compliance
Lightning Source LLC
Chambersburg PA
CBHW082149300426
44117CB00016B/2671